High School

A PRACTICAL GUIDE TO BETTER GRADES

by

George Weigand
East Carolina University
Greenville, North Carolina

Barron's
How to
Succeed
in High
School
A Practical Guide
to Better Grades
by George Weigand

English

AMERICAN HISTORY

BARRON'S EDUCATIONAL SERIES, INC.
Woodbury, New York • London • Toronto • Sydney

ACKNOWLEDGMENTS

THE AUTHOR WISHES TO ACKNOWLEDGE the very great contribution made by the hundreds of high school students who read and made suggestions concerning this book. He is especially grateful to his four sons who were so patient and so helpful in their suggestions and in proof reading. His wife, Mrs. Dorris Weigand is also due special thanks for her contribution to the drawings contained in this book.

Many other capable and interested persons were of great help in offering suggestions and in making contributions to the subject matter and general format of this manual:

Dr. B. Herbert Brown
Dr. Sidney Grollman
Mrs. Elizabeth Iseli
Mrs. Joyce Crisp
Dr. Aubrey C. Land
Mrs. Ila Myers
Mrs. Martha Patton
Dr. Philip Rovner
Mrs. Dorris Weigand
Miss Carol Woodard

The author is deeply grateful to all persons who contributed to this manual, especially those who offered encouragement and expended time and effort so unselfishly. But above all, the author wishes to restate his particular debt of gratitude to those students, both high school students and college students, who were of inestimable help in preparing the original manuscript.

CONTENTS

To each student who
would like to improve

To study (long hours) or not to study (long hours); that is the question.

Not too long ago Joe Zimmerman, a student in a good preparatory school, where the author was working as a consultant, brought up this problem:[1]

> I am a high school senior; I want to get into the University of ——————— and I have to get good grades in order to be admitted. But I'm going nuts studying – look at my study schedule—I don't have time for anything but studying, and I'm still not doing as well in school as I should. I don't have time for sports or dates. I really do want to go to college, but sometimes I wonder if it's worthwhile. If I have to study this hard in college I'll be a wreck in another couple of years. What in the world can I do? I'm in a mess.

What suggestions would you give to help this student? Do you think this is an isolated case?

Before we begin to solve this student's problem let us go back a few steps. For fifteen years the author worked with groups of students just out of high school (college freshmen). These students, you might be interested to know, were a very special kind of group. They were students who, for the most part, had not done well in high school, but who had decided to come to college (or as some of them said, "give college a try") even though they had poor scholastic backgrounds. With a little of the right kind of help many more of these students than we could hope for have gone on to graduate, and many have entered professional schools. What is the answer? No secrets, no tricks, and no magic; just a good job of learning how to learn *quickly* and *efficiently*, coupled with some understanding of *how* and *why* we learn.

You may wonder why college freshmen are used as exam-

[1] This incident is an actual case as are all other incidents cited in this book — only the names have been changed.

ples in a high school book. The answer is simple; the idea of writing a book to help high school students originated with these college freshmen. Over the years they have been saying, "If I had been taught how to study in high school I would never be in the mess I am in now." Many of them asked why something was not done to help high school students learn how to study.

The author decided to see how students who were still in high school felt about the idea of a study course. He talked with students from many different kinds of high schools. He was amazed at how many students said they would like to be doing better (in spite of the excuses they gave for not working) especially when they found that studying is relatively easy once one learns how and why to study. Not only did these students tell the author they wanted and needed a how-to-study book or course, they also told him what they thought should be in such a book or course.

The information gathered by the author about the need for increasing learning efficiency or learning how to study is also supported by Agatha Townsend in COLLEGE FRESHMEN SPEAK OUT (23). College Freshmen, in the book just cited list their biggest complaints as: not knowing how to study, not knowing how to take examinations, in fact, not knowing how to do most of the things taught in effective-study courses. These students have the ability but do not do as well as they feel they should do. What is the answer?

What have you got and how do you use it?

The answer is not how much you have, but how well you use it. The best illustration of this point is the example used at the beginning of this chapter. Here was a boy who knew what he wanted, had a definite goal, and had a reason for working; yet, he was experiencing much difficulty. He did not know how to use what he had. After being taught *how* to study, Joe earned better grades; yet, he was spending *less than half* the amount of time in studying he spent before he consulted with the author.

When this story is told to high school students they are immediately interested and want to know what suggestions were made. Frankly, it would take a small-sized book to explain what took place in those conferences, which is precisely what the author is doing — writing a short book on how to study efficiently.

How can this book help you?

The suggestions you will be given in the pages that follow have been tried and proved for many years. The author has taught effective-study methods at all academic levels from the high school level, through college level and even to graduate and professional-school levels. Students from ten years of age to seventy years of age have profited. Even some students who had received Law, Dental and Medical degrees have profited from learning how to study. Many of these students have expressed regret that they were not taught these effective-study methods and skills in high school.

This book will give you the *how's* as well as the *why's* of studying and learning. The author believes that each person has the right to know the reasons *why* before following any suggestions made to him. The methods suggested here are based on the best experimental evidence on how we learn, but the examples, so far as possible, will be taken from every-day life.

You will recognize many of the suggestions made in this book as being the same as those made by some of your better instructors. This book, however, will have the advantage of presenting, in a systematic fashion, most of the methods that good students have found to be most useful.

Are you doing as well as you would like to do in high school?

Regardless of what you think at the present moment, your high school grades will become a part of your permanent record. If you go no further than high school your grades will indicate to future employers something about your willingness and capacity to work. If you decide to go to college your grades will be the deciding factor, not only in which schools you will be eligible to enter, but whether you may enter at all.

As an average high school student you may not know or admit it, but if you fail to do as well as you would like to do in high school you fail for one of two practical reasons: you do not work, or you do not work efficiently. Of course, there are many reasons for not working, but we shall try at this point, to accent the positive and eliminate the negative and give you the practical techniques for succeeding in high school with the least effort.

If you are going to succeed you will have to meet certain requirements, regardless of the course or curriculum you select. You will be very interested in certain of these requirements, while others will be practically meaningless. If your school years are to be of any value to you, however, learn early in the game that any activity, sport, or job will have some parts which are distasteful. Take football as an example. Most players enjoy playing the game, but few enjoy doing the setting-up exercises and running around the track. If we compare school with athletics (which we shall do frequently) this book should help you to learn to live with the misery of setting-up exercises (your worst subjects) and help you to get the most enjoyment from playing the game (your favorite subjects). If we cannot appeal to you on this basis, let us try to convince you by saying that we can help you to get your school work finished sooner so that you will have more time for recreation.

How can you learn how to study?

At this point you probably think of studying as something entirely different from all other activities. There you are wrong; studying is a skill that can and must be developed just like any other skill. Studying can be compared with playing golf or tying your shoe laces — each skill requires practice to perfect it. This is a very important point. It means that you can become much more proficient in studying than you are right now. In fact, you can become good at studying and get good grades.

At times the topic of grades is a touchy one. The author has been told that some students who are capable and who should be on the honor roll avoid studying so they will not make it, while others feel that they get more attention when they fail. Other students are pressured so much to pass that they are satisfied with "just passing grades." Still others are supposed to be pressured by the "crowd" to do no better than just passing work. In talking with high school students, however, we find that while there are a few cases like the ones cited above, these pressures are overemphasized. The students themselves say that these are the excuses used by loafers; and, in fact, some of them admitted using these excuses. These students further state that if there are such pressures, any student can overcome them with practically no effort, if he really wants to do so.

There is a very real reason why many students do not work. They are afraid they will fail even if they do work. They consider themselves very practical, so they figure it is more sensible to fail or get low grades without working rather than get the same grades by working hard. If you fall into this latter category, read carefully. There are *very few* (if any) students who cannot or will not do at least fairly well if they work — *efficiently.* Do not worry too much about your "I.Q." or Scholastic Aptitude Rating. If you can tie your shoe laces, you can learn to study. If your "I.Q." were really low, chances are you would be in a special school. Ability is like a set of good muscles; neither is of much use in loafing, and neither will produce any results without work. "It ain't whatcha got but the way thatcha use it (worry less about your "I.Q." and emphasize your "I DO"); that's what gets results."

Introduction

What is your purpose in attending high school?

The chances are that you intend eventually to go into some kind of work or profession which will require a good educational background. Somewhere in the back of your mind you know you need an education. But have you ever really stopped to consider why *you* are attending high school?

Many of the high school students interviewed by the author answered the question of why attend high school by saying: "you have to go." But, when questioned further they admitted that they *needed* the education. Some said they really wanted to learn but were having difficulty. Most students, however, freely admitted that they were lackadaisical about putting forth the effort to get an education. Why should this be?

During the past few years the idea of going to high school and college has been taken for granted. Parents as well as students know, "in the back of their minds," that an education is necessary. Few people, however, really consider that our whole world of work, as well as our academic world, has become so complex that one must work and work hard to meet the increasing demands. In other words, everyone seems to be aware that an education is necessary but few seem to know *why!* We hear the statement: "people who have college educations make more money." But how often do you hear the statement the way it should be phrased: — those persons who are interested in the jobs or professions which pay the higher salaries need the education to qualify for these positions?

But there is still a more important factor. There are innumerable high school students who learn just because they enjoy learning and being well-informed. And there are countless others who could enjoy learning for learning's sake if they were taught how to learn, retain, and use the information available in our schools.

The problem of the reason for education.

Just a few years ago only a very limited segment of our population attended and/or completed high school and only the "elite" went to college. Now it is the commonly-accepted idea that everyone "just naturally" goes to high school, and, just as naturally goes on to college. It then comes as a rather rude shock to some parents that after their children complete high school that they "just naturally" are not admitted to the college of their choice — or any other college for that matter. Or, if their pride and joy does go to college that he does not do well. Parents as well as some students seem to feel that they are the victims of some form of discrimination. Seldom do they consider the fact that many high school graduates do not have the educational background to be admitted to college or to do the work once admitted.

Enough about what others think! What about you? What is your own personal reason for trying to get an education? Do you really understand that it is the education and learning necessary to earn a degree or diploma which are important and not the diploma itself? Do you ever really consider what you can get out of school or just the fact that attending school is something you have to do to satisfy your parents and the local truant officer? Just what is *your* purpose in attending school?

Five years ago the writer might have been trying to convince you that you should have a well-defined vocational objective to help make your studies meaningful. Further investigation, however, shows that the world of work has become so complicated and so demanding that high school students cannot possibly know enough about the various opportunities to make a decision. In addition, high school students may not know enough about their own aptitudes and interests to be able to apply these characteristics most appropriately.

High school, then, should be for you a place where you not only learn a series of courses but also a place where you can develop your interests and talents. You can learn and sharpen up your skills in the three R's which are *an absolute necessity* in any area. In addition, you have the opportunity to explore the world of science, history, languages and many other areas. Each class, each instructor should represent to you a challenge and an opportunity. If you do your best in each class you give yourself the chance to see how well you can develop your interests and abilities in a number of areas.

What practical use is a high school education?

It is sometimes difficult to convince high school students that what they are learning is practical even though the evidence to prove the case is overwhelming. If you stop to think, you will realize that what you are being taught in school is for future use. Whether you are going to work immediately after high school or you are going on to college, you will find what you are learning to be of immense practical value. Even the person who learns for the sheer joy of learning uses what he learns. But let us look at *the* practical use of your education.

While there are literally thousands of cases of individuals like the student who was given a "better summer job" because he had learned to read blue prints in high school, the most practical value of the education you are now getting is the fact that it is a base on which you can add and eventually become really educated. And, without that base you cannot progress.

What good is a high school education?

Tom Ballinger and his father visited the author, told a sad story, and asked a question. Tom had just failed out of the College of Engineering and wanted to know what he could do — what was his next step! After a long discussion it was decided that Tom did not have the background to do the work required in engineering. It was a difficult decision, but after much discussion Tom agreed to take the author's advice and go to a preparatory school to get the background he so badly needed.

After several months of preparatory work, Tom returned to college and again took up the study of the same very difficult engineering program. Tom earned a "C+" average for his first semester and a "B" average for the second term. In talking with Tom, the author heard one statement repeated over and over in a number of different ways: "If only I hadn't wasted so much time when I was in high school — if I had only learned, really learned the fundamentals the first time I'd never have wasted so much time."

Tom is just one example of literally hundreds the author could cite. Literally thousands of students, both in high school *and* college, find to their sorrow that they do not have the background to pass the courses they are taking. Many students are discouraged from taking second-year mathematics, languages and many other subjects simply because they do not have the backgrounds. Many potential scientists fall by the wayside, *not* because they do not have the ability but because they do not have the basic knowledge or learning on which to build.

The purpose of this book.

Right now you have, as was pointed out before, the opportunity to explore and learn about a great variety of subject-matter areas. If you follow the suggestions given in the book you will find that learning can actually be fun as well as rewarding — you will be shown how to learn well *with the least amount of effort*. Make no mistake, however, no one can learn without working. You do not learn by *osmosis*. But most of us find that working is enjoyable when we can see positive results.

This book will show you methods of learning, really learning what you are being taught. You will then be rather pleasantly surprised to find that you will be able to *use* what you have learned. You will then be able to add what you *are* learning to what you *have* learned. In this way you will begin to acquire the education (not merely passing courses) you are working for and for which you will have to pay in both time and money. In addition, you will sharpen your work habits and study skills to the point that whether you go to college or decide on some other form of higher education you will have the skills so essential for success.

CHAPTER **I**

You and the World of School and Work

Introduction

The area of vocational selection and vocational guidance becomes increasingly difficult when we consider the fact that the jobs many of you will be working at after you finish school are not even in existence today — so how can we choose or prepare for such jobs? There is also the fact that we are too often influenced by some agency or other. Within the space of a few years we have seen the opinions of the people in our nation's capital change considerably. A few years ago our youth was being told in substance that everyone should go to college. This idea was amplified by private industry which wanted more and more engineers, mathematicians etc. Today our friends in Washington are singing the praises of a two-year, technical-school education. Quite a change!

Which of the opinions is correct? The answer is neither is correct or incorrect, the whole idea is wrong! Our emphasis should be on the individual, where he can make his greatest contribution and what will be best for him. The emphasis in this chapter will be on *you* and how *you* can discover things about yourself and the world of work which will enable you to make some meaningful decisions about yourself. Such an emphasis will allow you to make meaningful decisions about the area of work or kind of work you would like to do. If you are employed in the appropriate area of work and have reasonable education and training you will be in a position to be considered for those jobs which are not even in existence today. But, please remember this chapter is not for reading — it is for thinking about and for working on. The decisions you make will affect not only your school work but your career.

Our whole society is influenced by ideas of instant everything from coffee to success. Please try to remember that the choice of an occupation or way of life is one of the most important decisions you will ever make. Please, take time to think.

Part I. Goals and the Reason for Working

What is your purpose in working?

Suppose you were taken to the edge of a very dense jungle and asked to walk due North for ten miles as quickly as you could. Suppose further that you had been given all the training necessary to go through jungle terrain quickly and efficiently. How fast do you think you would be moving after the first mile or two, if indeed you even started?

Suppose you were given the same instructions and the same training. In this case, however, you were told other students were starting from different points, and the first person to travel the ten miles would be given a new sports car with all speed equipment and accessories already installed. How fast do you think you would be moving by the end of the tenth mile?

In the second case there is a reason for starting and finishing fast. In the first case there is no real good reason for starting unless you just happen to like walking through jungles. Maybe no one is going to offer you a sports car for walking ten miles, but the example does illustrate the point that each of us must have a good reason for expending effort. In the same way you should have a good reason for studying, but it must be *your* reason. It is possible to explain how to study without knowing why, but the explanation would be about as effective as asking you to walk through ten miles of jungle without giving you a reason.

What is your incentive (reason) for studying?

In the illustration given at the beginning of this section the sports car would serve as an incentive for most students. But there is something inside you that makes the car appeal to you, and we call that something *motivation*. What do you want out of life? What goal is there for you on the other side of the "Blackboard Jungle?" Will this goal bring you happiness and satisfaction or just drudgery?

Eventually each of us wants to make a place for himself and to be happy in life. To accomplish this we *must* work. What will your work be — merely a way to make a living? Or will you choose a job you will enjoy and which will give you satisfaction in addition to your daily bread? Just stop for a moment and consider that if you work only eight hours a day you will be spending one-third of your life at your job! Why not choose something that you will enjoy doing, something that will give you satisfaction!

Now do you see the tie-in? If the goal you choose (the incentive on the other side of the jungle) is appealing to you, you will be motivated to do the work; in addition, the work will be relatively easy. If you have no real goal or no appealing goal, the work will be drudgery, or perhaps you will not work at all. *What is your goal? Ask yourself these questions:*

1] What am I going to do after I finish school?

2] If I could ask for and get (right now) any job I *wanted* (and automatically or magically got all the training and qualifications for that job) what would I choose?

3] What do I *really* know about the job I have chosen? What is the work I like, and what will I be doing (what operations will I perform?) in that job?

4] What and how much can my high school education contribute to my success in my future job?

Why worry about jobs now?

The main reason is that your future job represents one goal you should be working toward right now. Your future job is the thing which can make your education meaningful. But many students feel they are too young to think about jobs. They think that some bolt from the blue will help them to decide, or they are completely unrealistic about the occupations they choose.

One high school counselor made the following statements:

> I often talk with students just to learn about what they expect to do after school. Often, especially in the tenth grade, but also in the twelfth, students are still soaring imaginatively to the college farthest away, to the glamour job, to a self-sacrificing-help-others occupation. They don't listen if you try to bring their dreams in line with reality.

When do people stop this soaring off to romantic occupations? Well, some students never do. They never even *try* to choose a goal which will be both realistic and satisfying. When we ask high school graduates (those who will attend college) what they are going to do after they graduate from college, too often we hear them say, "I don't know," or "I just haven't given it much thought." Then there are other students who change their occupational choices as often as they change their shirts. On the other hand, when the importance of a goal is pointed out, most students finally decide they need help in selecting the occupation in which they can be happy and successful.

Where do you stand right now as far as knowing what you want out of life? What do you want to do for a living? Both high school and college students agree that everyone should *begin* to look into the matter of occupations while he is|was still in high school. Are you one of those students who is "soaring imaginatively" to the University of the Hula Islands, or who wants to be an actor, a whaler, or the president of General Motors? Have you chosen or are you choosing a job which *suits* you, or one which pleases your unrealistic dreams and imagination? Have you chosen or even thought about your future occupation?

How do you choose a job realistically?

The first thing you must realize is that no one is going to tailor a job to fit you; you must fit the job. Each position naturally requires a certain amount of ability, but ability is only part of the picture. Your personality and interest must also be suitable. Let us look at one example. Hank Smith was a rather bright boy who had always done well both in school and in athletics. When he was with people he knew well he was a rather good talker. His parents and friends convinced him that with his brains and ability to talk he "could make a million in the 'selling racket'." When Hank talked to the author he mentioned these facts, but, in addition, he said he had always liked to work with young people. He had coached boys' teams for the playground leagues, and had even done a little tutoring (on his own). He said he would really like to be a teacher and coach, but his father wanted him to go into business. Hank added that although he was considered a "good talker" he was actually shy with "new people" and not at all aggressive in a sales sense.

Hank's case is not unusual; there are many which are similar. Students often choose or are pushed into jobs where they have neither the personality nor the interest to do well.

To choose a job realistically you will have to take *all of you* into consideration — your abilities, your personality, and your interest. And only you know all about yourself. The task here is to get you to look at yourself, get to know yourself, and find out what area of work you really fit.

What are your real qualities, abilities, and interests? To what extent do you consider or have you considered <u>yourself</u> in selecting a goal?

The chances are that you will need quite a bit of information about yourself and your surroundings (environment) before you can answer these questions to your own satisfaction. You, one complete individual, are the result of a lot of things — your parents and their training, the friends with whom you have worked and played, your education, and thousands upon thousands of other experiences. As a result of all these experiences you have developed certain of your abilities, your personality, and your interests. You like certain things and dislike others; you do some things well and others not so well. In other words, you have done a lot of learning. Let us try to put as much of your experience and learning to work for you as is humanly possible. But remember, the final decision should be yours. Listen to your parents, teachers, and friends, and consider their suggestions, but do not allow yourself to be pushed or forced into something you know you will not fit. Do not turn out to be the proverbial square (peg in a round hole.) In the next section of this chapter you will be given some help in evaluating your qualities, abilities, and interests.

PART II.   Fitting Your Qualities, Abilities, and Interests into the World of School and Work

How good are you really?

Some time ago a student came into the author's office and complained about being placed in a reading class. "I read 600 words a minute and have a comprehension score of 95," (i.e., he understood 95% of what he read, which is a very fine score) he said, "and I can't see wasting my time when I read twice as well as most students." The author talked with him and finally convinced him that he should try to work up to his own level; if he could read 600 words a minute with no help he could certainly improve with help and direction. Some three months later the same student stopped the author in the hall and said, "You know, you were right; I'm now reading 1100 words a minute and still have a 95 in comprehension."

Is this an unusual story? Not at all. It happens every day in reading classes throughout the country. Each of us has qualities and abilities, but very few of us ever really develop them. Why is this? Because most of us never look at ourselves to see how we can improve, and most of us have a tendency to take ourselves and our *real* abilities too lightly.

Ask yourself: What are my real qualities? What can I do to improve?

One of your first tasks in looking at yourself is to learn what sort of person you really are and what you want out of life. It is sometimes difficult for a person to be honest with himself; you will really have to try. Find out what you really want to do, then learn how to do it. Remember, no one can find fault with you for wanting to improve or for wanting to be a better person.

Have you thought about your real qualities? Possibly the improvement-in-reading example at the beginning of this section made no impression on you, but it is easy to prove that you too have more ability than you usually use. Think of the number of times you have tried to complete a study assignment without any success. Then your teacher announced an examination. Isn't it strange how quickly you were able to complete the assignment! There was no lack of ability, but just a lack of what we have already pointed out — motivation. Ability is like the engine of a car or like a sewing machine; it does nothing until someone starts it, and it performs no service until someone guides it and directs it. You also know that some drivers can get much more performance from a car than can other drivers. Some people keep their cars well tuned; others let them fall apart. Some girls make very attractive clothes on very ancient sewing machines; other girls with the most modern equipment produce nothing. Students are the same with ability as drivers are with cars or girls are with sewing machines. Some are able to perform well with very little equipment (ability) while others who have the best in equipment (considered "very bright") flunk out of school.

At this point, how well are you doing in school? You have already learned in the previous section that if you are an average student and are not doing as well as you would like to do, you can blame one or two reasons: you do not work, or you do not work efficiently. Let us look at the reasons for not working. (The remainder of this book will show you how to work efficiently.) Some students say, "I'm just plain lazy." Is this so? There are some people who are not inclined to work (at some things), and there are those who have difficulties which make it almost impossible for them to work (effectively). Both are serious problems and merit consideration. Too many parents and teachers often fail to recognize that for a student to perform well he must physically be able to perform. Consequently, the author strongly suggests that every student have a complete dental and medical check-up, including a *thorough* eye examination, at least once each year. To give you some insight into our reasons for this suggestion we mention the fact that in one of our surveys we had eye check-ups given to a group of students who had not done well in high school. The check-ups revealed that thirty percent of those students who needed glasses did not have them.

Why not begin to take stock of yourself? Is it that you are not inclined to work, or is it that one or two other problems are bothering you? Possibly a desire to do something else draws you away from your (school) work. Perhaps you do well in some things and in some courses, but not very well in others. The chances are you will admit you can work like a beaver on some things while other tasks leave you completely cold. The problem then boils down to a matter of interests. If you are interested enough in a given job you will work at it. Right?

Evaluate your qualities, abilities, and interests.

Just what are some of the things which can get you moving and make you work? What do you like to do? What are the things you *think* you would like to do? *Your* experiences, *your* education, and *your* training have given and are giving you the bases for your likes, dislikes, interests, and desires, and only you can tell what they are. But you will probably have to do a little work before you recognize your likes, dislikes, and interests.

We would like you to answer the next few questions as best you can. Do not be discouraged if you cannot answer them to your own satisfaction. One purpose of these questions is to orient your thinking and to help you find out what information you will need.

5] How did you answer questions 1–4 on page **15** of this section? (compare your answers with those of Phil Stanley's shown on page **22**)

6] What would you most like to be doing:

(a) right now?

(b) right now as a *daily job* or *occupation?*

7] How much more training (education) will you need to get the job you want?

8] What is the employment outlook in your chosen field?

9] Where can you get additional information, applications, etc.?

10] Suppose something were to happen which would make it impossible for you to get the job you really want. What would be your second choice?

Perhaps you would like to know the reasons for these questions. First, we would like for you to begin thinking about what you are going to do after you finish school and how much education you will need. Second, you know that we work better if we are doing something we like to do. Third, it was found in a study of college students that *successful* students had chosen jobs and school subjects which were in line with what *they would most like to do.* So, from the point of view of what you would most like to do, evaluate your answers. In an ideal case your chosen job would be the same as what you would most like to do. For example, if you said you would *most* like to be an engineer, and you have decided to become a chemical engineer, you are on the right track. If you have decided to become a chemist because you cannot attend a school which offers chemical engineering, you are still on the right track. But if you have decided to become a surgeon, a jet test pilot, or an FBI investigator, your occupational train has just been derailed.

Take the case of Phil Stanley who was interviewed as part of the study mentioned above. Before the study was begun the author had the opportunity to talk with Phil about his poor performance in school. It was rumored that Phil's father had promised him a prestige model convertible if he would get a 2.0 ("C") average for one semester. Phil said that his father had promised him the car and when asked how he could explain his poor performance he gave the following quote: "I won't work more than a half hour a night for nobody, for nothin', nohow."

In spite of what was said in the conversation reported above, Phil said that he did want an education but that he was not interested in getting an education. The contradictions were solved when Phil took part in the author's study. The answers to the questions on page 3 supplied the solution.

In answer to question 2, Phil said he wanted more than anything else in the world to become a forester.

Question 1 brought out the fact that Phil's father had decided that Phil would work in the family's bed-spring factory and become a business tycoon.

Question 3 — Phil hated the bed-spring business.

Question 4 — Phil had decided on sociology as his area of "major interest."

Under the circumstances, what chance do you think Phil had of succeeding either in the bed-spring factory OR in school?

Why should you choose one occupation when there is something you would much rather do? Is it because someone advised or pressured you to choose a particular job (because you have the hands of a surgeon), because the work (you think) is easy, or because you do not have anything better to do? The questions you have already answered about the amount of education needed in your chosen occupation and your most desired occupation are extremely important. Well-meaning friends and relatives will advise you, but on what basis? How do these people know your real interests, desires, and abilities? They do not do the work or suffer the heartaches of failure, you do. If you want to get help, talk to your guidance counselor and to your instructors. Let them *help* you with your plans.

What do you do if you have no chosen occupation?

If you have no chosen occupation or you have no idea of what you would like to do, take a look at your interests, aptitudes, and abilities. If you really look at yourself you will find many interests and aptitudes which should help you in the choice of a job or profession. Again, your counselor can be of real help in this area. But remember one thing. Real and effective counseling is hard work for you and the counselor. No counselor can honestly answer the questions "What should I do?" or "What should I be?" for you. And no counselor can be of much help if you go to see him only because you are forced to go. You must have an honest desire for assistance, and you must give the counselor something with which to work.

In order to get information which will be of value to a counselor, please try to answer the items which follow:

11] What kinds of things do you like to do?

12] What kinds of things do you dislike doing?

13] What kinds of things do you do well?

14] Describe something you did which gave you a great deal of satisfaction and made you feel good.

15] Describe something you did which made you feel miserable.

16] Check back over items 12–16 and see how many references you made to hobbies, jobs and school subjects.

17] Re-do items 11–15, first keeping jobs in mind (e.g., item 13; what jobs have you done well?) then keeping subjects in mind (e.g., item 11, what subject or course do you like?).

Where do you fit in the occupational scheme?

At this point you probably fit into one of three categories: (1) you have no idea; (2) you have an idea but are not quite sure; (3) you know exactly what you are going to do after school. Regardless of where you fit, the following sections and questions will be of value to you. If you have decided further training is a necessity, there are thousands of colleges and technical schools you might attend. How definite are your plans, and how did you arrive at them? Do you or did you have enough facts to make the best choice? Let us look at the student who has decided to go to work after finishing high school. Perhaps you think you have no worries as far as a job is concerned. You know you can take over your father's bagel bakery, or your uncle who is a fast-talking lawyer can get you a job with the FBI, or your maiden aunt who owns stock in an aircraft company will get you a job as a test pilot, etc., etc. It *could* be that you have no worries! But the chances are you are in for a real let-down. The person who chooses a job on the basis of reasons similar to those just given or who "soars imaginatively" usually knows nothing about the basic requirements of the job. So, regardless of whether you have chosen an occupation, *you need information.*

First, why does anyone choose a certain kind of work? He likes the work; it is easy; he does not know about other kinds of jobs; he wants prestige, money, or power! But basically, there are two main reasons why each of us needs to work: (1)

to support ourselves and our families, and (2) to feel that we are productive and serve some real purpose in life (satisfaction). Those of us who are wise or lucky, or both, have positions in which we accomplish both of these aims. What about you? Will you be able to accomplish both aims?

Is money all you need?

Do not kid yourself at this point by thinking that as long as you have a job which pays plenty of money you will be happy. The psychiatrists' couches are overworked by people with such thoughts. The remainder of the people who get little or no relaxation or satisfaction from their work keep the stomach-ulcer experts in business. Each of us has to feel that he gets some personal satisfaction from life, and that means life — not just some small part of life. Whether your job be teacher, lawyer, doctor, homemaker, beautician, electrician, plumber, or disc jockey you will want to feel that you are good at your job. You will need satisfaction, and you will want to know that you are living, not just existing.

What information will you need to choose a job you will fit?

First, you should know something about your abilities, how well you use them, and what kinds of jobs these abilities will fit. Your counselor will be able to help you with the answers to these problems *after* you get certain other facts. Think back over the answers you gave to items 11–17. If you were unable to come up with any good answers, start checking yourself to see what you do enjoy doing. (It might help you to make a list of these things.) When you consider what you enjoy doing, list the kinds of work you like doing, such as working in the library, filing, typing, carpentry, building model airplanes, designing, serving, etc. Also list the subjects you enjoy, such as English, mathematics, science, shop, etc. Do not try to list occupations such as dentistry or engineering; concentrate on what *operations* or *tasks* you like to do. Now make a list of the things and subjects you *dislike*.

You should now be in a position to talk with your counselor or favorite instructor. The combination of information you will be able to supply and some information on your abilities and how much better you might do if you used them should put you on the path of finding the job which will be right for you.

Now what do you know about your job?

Sometimes we know what we want but not how to go about getting it. Take the case of the boy who consulted the author at change-of-major time. The young man said that he wanted to become a psychiatrist but became quite abusive when he was assigned a pre-medical program. An explanation was made concerning the training of a psychiatrist at which point the student made no bones about the fact that he doubted the author's sanity. Finally, another approach was tried. The student was asked to describe the kind of work he would be doing as a psychiatrist and he gave an excellent description of a personnel manager's position. The student was quite happy when he was given a business program with a major in personnel. But when he left he still insisted he was going to become a psychiatrist.

Here is the kind of information you will need to help you to decide whether a given job will be right for you.

18] How much money do you need to live the way you want to live? Does your chosen job pay that much?

19] Describe the working conditions in your chosen job (or the job you would like) with reference to:

    (a) duties to be performed
    (b) starting job, e.g., apprenticeship
    (c) advancement possibilities
    (d) hours per week

    (e) daily hours
    (f) employment trends (is the number of jobs increasing or decreasing?)
    (g) steady or seasonal work
    (h) difficulty of the work physically and mentally
    (i) compulsory Union membership
    (j) inside (office) or outside work
    (k) amount of social life connected with the job (e.g., how much entertaining, lecturing, joining clubs will you have to do, or be expected to do?)

20] What are the basic requirements for your job in so far as the following are concerned:

    (a) age
    (b) physical requirements
    (c) minimum education
    (d) special training (e.g., technical school) needed, or needed for advancement
    (e) bonding

21] What are the company benefits?

    (a) How paid?
    (b) Bonuses, overtime, extra pay?
    (c) Hospitalization, life insurance, social security, retirement plan?
    (d) Starting salary, top salary?
    (e) How much money can you reasonably expect to make after five years? After ten years? After fifteen years?
    (f) What are the provisions for vacations and sick leave (with pay, without pay, etc.)?
    (g) Does company pay for special training?

22] After you have answered these questions your work has only begun. Keep your information up to date and reevaluate as you learn more; keep inquiring.

PART III.　Getting to Know Yourself

How much do you really know about yourself at this point?

Perhaps after learning about positions you wonder just where and how you fit into the scheme of things. Perhaps after taking a kind of preliminary look at yourself you have decided there are a few things which you should change. But do you know enough about yourself to know what changes should be made? On the other hand, you might think of yourself as being quite independent and not caring what others think of you. If you are of that opinion, please consider this for a moment. Have you tried to impress anyone lately? What about the cute little gal or the good-looking boy who drives the convertible? Or why do you think you "dug out" so fast when the traffic light turned green? Could you have slouched just a bit more than usual and looked just a bit more sullen to impress Miss Galaxy, the astronomy lab instructor, with how little you care and how "tough" or "sharp" (or whatever the popular word is) you are? Each of us has done something, and recently, to impress *someone.*

No one is implying that you should change and become another person. We are simply saying that each of us has tried to impress people, and when we are honest we admit that we want people to like us and pay attention to us. Some of us, however, are a bit clumsier than others, and when our efforts fail to gain recognition we take the I-don't-care attitude. But we prove we do care by getting our attention by being sullen, by being a wise-guy, or by being a trouble maker. Remember, *you* choose your own way of impressing people.

Let us put these ideas into a more practical form. Consider that you and one of your classmates apply for the same job. You both have the same education and the same grades. What will the employer use to help him choose the one who gets the job? In the event your classmate is not the boss's nephew, the personnel man will consider appearances, how well each applicant expresses himself and handles himself, interest expressed and shown in the job, attitudes, and general, overall impression. In some cases both applicants will have to take tests, the results of which will be used to help make a decision. If the test results are similar, the personnel man will choose the person who makes the better impression and the better appearance. At this time will the *real* you make the impression, or will the personnel manager see a lot of affected mannerisms?

Let's take stock of you!

Have you ever considered how your behavior and appearance affect others and influence your whole life? Think for a minute; are you satisfied? If not, don't worry. Find out how you affect others. Take an honest look at the things you do. If you are doing the best you can, enough said. But if you feel you should improve, and you really want to improve, all you have to do is capitalize on your good points and play down those characteristics you feel are less desirable. Of course, you will need to know which of your traits annoy others as well as the things people like about you. Chances are that only a few things will have to be changed, and probably small changes at that. So take inventory!

23] Write a brief sketch of yourself emphasizing what you think are your good points and your bad points.

24] Which of your characteristics would you have to change to become:

(a) more likeable?
(b) a better student?
(c) a more desirable friend (acquaintance)?
(d) more desirable as an employee?
(e) more desirable at social affairs?
(f) *more satisfied with yourself?*

25] What do you do when someone:

 (a) asks you to explain something to him?
 (b) asks you to speak before a class (group)?
 (c) pays you a compliment?
 (d) does something you feel deserves a compliment?
 (e) criticizes you?

26] List the kinds of things said about you (good and bad) which give you some idea about the kind of person you are:

 (a) by your parents
 (b) by your teachers
 (c) by your friends (same sex)
 (d) by your friends (opposite sex)

27] List the suggestions or statements made to you by others (teachers, parents, clergyman, doctor, dentist) which give indications of how you appear or how you could improve.

28] To what groups, organizations, and churches do your friends belong? Do you belong?

29] How do your actions differ when you are with your parents? When you are at a social gathering? When you are on a date?

30] How many times have you volunteered or been elected or delegated to lead a group?

31] Rate yourself on how well you can take a joke (and be honest).

32] Rate yourself on:

 (a) your ability to tell jokes or stories
 (b) how often friends go out of their way to tell you a joke or story
 (c) how often you are willing to go out of your way to do a favor for a friend, acquaintance, teacher, your parents

    (d) how often you are willing to do a job which will benefit others, but which is distasteful to you

    (e) your loyalty to parents, friends, and school

33] How often do you make unkind remarks about your parents, your friends, or your school?

34] How do you choose what clubs or organizations you will join?

35] When you are discussing a matter or just arguing, how much do you seem to enjoy pressing a point or question for the sake of embarrassing the other person?

36] How often do you do things because "everyone else does it?"

37] How many hours per week do you watch television alone, with your family, with friends?

38] What do you do when someone bumps into you in the hallway, elevator, etc.?

39] What do you do when you bump into someone in the hallway, elevator, etc.?

If you have really tried to answer items 23 to 39 you have no doubt found out quite a few things about yourself. If you simply read the questions, observe yourself during the next few weeks and see how you do react. Many of us are guilty of what is called *projecting*, i.e., saying another person has the faults we ourselves have. But regardless of what we find, each of us will have some good points and some bad ones. We will also find that none of us is completely different. Some of our friends will have many of the characteristics we possess. Observe these characteristics in others and see what effect they have. Now you will be in a better position to play up your good points and play down or eliminate the traits that you yourself feel are undesirable. You might begin by giving the other person the benefit of the doubt. Consider that he is as nice a person as you think you are.

If you have tried seriously to complete this chapter you will want to summarize what you know about yourself. Start by asking yourself this question: "Do I really have a set of standards to guide my actions, or do I let the group set standards for me?" One example of changing standards often mentioned by high school students is honesty. Many students tell us that they do not take things which do not belong to them; yet they admit that under certain circumstances they give or get help on tests. Why? "Because everyone else does it," they say. When we do things which are contrary to *our own* standards we have good reason to be dissatisfied with ourselves. If you are going to develop into the kind of person *you* want to be, develop enough intestinal fortitude to do what you think is best, whether it be in choosing a club or fraternity, a steady date, or a job.

Now for the important task of summarizing all aspects of you.

40] What is your chosen job?

41] How many of the qualifications necessary for success in that job do you possess?

42] How much education does the job require?

43] What are your educational plans?

44] How well do your talents and interests line up with your chosen job?

45] Now combine all the information you have gathered about yourself and write a brief sketch of yourself emphasizing:

(a) your good points
(b) your undesirable characteristics
(c) how *you* think you should change to become the person you would like to be
(d) how you think you can become better at dealing with others

If you have been unable to answer the items listed earlier in this section, items 40 to 45 will be difficult indeed. Most students will have to work *hard* to arrive at a complete set of answers which will satisfy them. The main question now is:

46] How well are you satisfied with the information you have about yourself?

Whether you are satisfied or dissatisfied, you still have a long way to go if this area of work is to be of any real value to you. You will have to continue to look at yourself objectively, and continue to check any major decisions you will have to make. As time goes on you will learn new things, hear of new and different jobs, and see new opportunities. In an interview, Peter Drucker, one of the country's top management consultants emphasized the point of continual searching for new opportunities by indicating that even he did not know what he wanted to be when he grew up. Do not let yourself down by failing to consider any new opportunity in light of what you know about yourself. Also, many things will change — your interests, desires, and opinions of yourself. In other words, you will grow and develop. If your interests and desires do change, look around for new and more suitable goals. *You* are the center in this orientation. The information and work sheets are merely a guide for *your* use. Use them for your own benefit.

CHAPTER **2**

Planning Your Studies
and Recreation

How much do you know
about when and where you should study?

Let us test you on your knowledge of when and where to study. Please mark the following statements with a "T" if you think they are true, and an "F" if you think they are false.

1] The *best* time to study is immediately after school.

2] The best time to study is after dinner.

3] It is a wise idea to *plan* to see your favorite television program, even though it interferes with your studies.

4] Most students can study better with a radio playing their favorite kind of music in the background.

5] A person really needs a "real study room" in order to be able to study effectively.

6] It is best to study when and what you feel like studying, rather than planning in advance what and when you will study.

7] It is absolutely worthless to try to study for ten or fifteen minutes at a time.

8] To be a *real* student a person has to cut down on his recreational activities and spend most of his time studying.

34

9] Most students spend much more time in worthwhile recreational activities than they realize.

It may sound strange, but you should have marked each one of the preceding questions as false, except Question 3. From past experience the author knows that practically all parents and many teachers will disagree with him concerning the answers to most of these questions, but he is relatively certain that you will agree with him after you have completed the following section. As you read through this section, refer back to the questions and re-answer them in light of what you learn.

How much do you accomplish in the time you spend studying? Consider the following illustration:

Margie is seated at her father's desk with her school books. "This is terrible; four algebra problems to work tonight. Mr. Johnson explained in class how to do them, but I didn't know what he was saying. Let's see; maybe I can do this first one. Mother, don't you think Mr. Johnson is just awful expecting me to do four whole algebra problems when I don't expect I'll ever have to use any of this stuff? I wonder if Nancy is going to the dance. I know I'll just die if Bill doesn't ask me to go. Golly, it makes me hungry to work so hard." (Margie leaves for a "few minutes" and returns with a sandwich and a cold drink.) "Maybe Nancy can help me with these problems." (Margie dials the telephone.) "Hello, Nancy. This is Margie. Can you do the algebra problems Mr. Johnson gave us for homework? I don't see what a square has to do with algebra. Oh, *that* kind of square. Speaking of squares, do you think Charles will break down and ask Susan to . . . oh, can you hear the radio? Do you have it turned on, too? Isn't that real dreamy music? Say, I have the cutest new dress . . . (etc.) . . . Well, goodbye now." (Margie looks at her algebra book a minute, and then at the desk clock.) "Mother, I've been working at this algebra problem for an hour and a half, and I just can't get it. When I tell Mr. Johnson I worked this long he won't believe me, but you know I did, don't you, Mother?"

Unusual? Not at all; it happens all the time, and not just with high school students. Counselors in colleges and supervisors in business constantly bemoan the fact that people just do not use their time or do not know how to make the best use of their time. In fact, most people do not know how to get any real results for the effort they expend!

The conditions under which Margie was attempting to study are not unusual, either. The telephone was handy, the radio was playing in the background, and there were "things" to remind her of dates and dances. Most people have pet theories about studying and/or concentrating. Too many people believe and want to believe that radios and other distractions are absolutely necessary to help them to concentrate.

The problem of the study habits of young people and the question about background music for studying has become so acute that it attracted the attention of a nationally-known columnist. Bill Gold, in his column, "The District Line," in the *Washington Post and Times Herald*, reported that a friend of his came home from work one evening and noticed his son's door was closed. Angrily, he asked his wife, "Why isn't that boy doing his homework?" When his wife asked how he knew their son was *not* studying, he snapped, "Because he doesn't have his radio turned on."

One high school student summed up the prevailing opinion of quite a few students when he said, "I find that I can't study unless I have a radio playing; I need *something* like that to help me to concentrate and to keep me from becoming bored." Do you agree with this idea?

What are the facts about "noise" in the background? Instead of looking to pet theories about radios and the like, let us consult with the professor who does research on this topic. What does he say? The professor would tell us that distractions (he could call them "irrelevant stimuli") such as radios playing in the background, pictures, etc., tend to help us to concentrate or hinder us from concentrating *according to what we believe they will do.* "So there," you say, "the professor supports *my* idea." But just a minute! There are at least two things wrong. First, if you need more than your studies to "occupy your mind," your studies are not absorbing enough, or, more likely, *you are not absorbed in your studies.* The chances are you are merely reading, not studying. But perhaps this argument means nothing. You still "study better" with the latest popular (or soft classical) music playing in the background. After all, the man who does the research said it could help. True, but you have not heard all of the evidence. The professor would also tell us that when we work with distractions in the background we become *more tired* doing a given amount of work than if we worked without these distractions. Take an example all of you have experienced. You begin to add a long column of figures. On the third or fourth column (carrying 4) a friend interrupts you with, "Hey, Pete." You try to ignore him and continue adding. He does not know you are busy, so he calls again. Now what happens? You begin to add aloud, pointing and *pressing* the paper with your pencil so you will not lose your place. In other words, by talking, pointing, and pressing you are using *more energy* to add the column of figures than you would ordinarily use.

The amount of extra energy used can actually be measured. In one experiment, which you may have seen in popular magazine advertisements for accoustical tiles, the work of a group of secretaries was checked under usual office conditions and under quiet conditions. The experimenter checked carefully to see how much work each girl produced and how many errors she made. In the meantime, little measuring devices were attached to the typewriters to see how hard the keys were pressed. From this measure of how hard the keys were pressed the experimenter could show *how hard* each girl had to work to produce a certain amount of work — the harder the pressure, the more work.

In the first part of the experiment the girls were checked in their usual office conditions. In the second part of the experiment everything was the same *except* that the office had been quieted down considerably by the use of accoustical tiles. What were the results? The girls produced the same amount of work and made the same number of errors in both parts of the experiment, BUT, under the noisy conditions they worked much, much harder to produce the same amount of work. Under quiet conditions the girls even reported that they felt less tired at the end of the day, were able to enjoy dates and other recreational activities more, felt better about coming to work the next day, and, in general, felt better.

After all of this, how can an average student like you find a good place in which to study? The answer is very simple. *Choose a place where you do nothing but study.* "Great," you say, "but where do I find such a place? Where do I get the accoustical tiles, etc.?" Students who ask these questions are usually thinking of a "book-lined study" similar to the Duke of Webfoot's study which was pictured in a recent issue of *Hilarious Living.* A place for studying does not have to be fancy. The *easiest* way to get a study nook is to select an unused corner of a room in your home where there are no distractions. Choose a spot that has no associations for you, a place you have not used previously for pleasure reading, writing letters, listening to the radio, hobbies, etc. Now, make up your mind that this place will be used *only* for study. Also, there is no need to worry about fancy equipment. You do not need all the equipment pictured in the popular magazines. Of course, a good desk and chair are desirable, and you should have a good, INDIRECT lamp, but you can rig up your own substitutes. A smooth board between two supports will serve as a desk, and a half-gallon can will make a fine indirect lamp. On the other hand, many teenagers seem to prefer a gadget called a "study board" or "reading board" such as the one pictured in the illustration Figure 1. Use your own ingenuity. But select a place where you will not be disturbed. By the way, do not neglect to consider your homeroom, the school library, or empty classrooms for short study sessions while at school. (We are going to talk about these short study sessions later in this chapter when we discuss when to study.) You now have the basic idea of *where* to study. There is only one more thing to remember as far as equipment is concerned: take all the material necessary to complete a given assignment to your study place *before* you begin to study. In this way a great deal of time

FIG. 1 *Illustration showing student using study board.*

will be saved, but in addition you will not have to interrupt your studies and your thinking to get additional equipment. As a consequence, you will be able to concentrate better and get more done in less time.

When should you study?

Bill had been given an extra assignment in English which would take at least two and one-half hours of work, and which was due the next day. He had football practice until 4:40 and a band practice from 7:30 to 9:00, plus an additional half-hour of travel time each way. Should Bill try to do some of his homework before or after football practice? Should he try to do all of his homework when he comes home from band practice? Should he *go* to band practice? What would you advise Bill to do?

The Professor's standard answer would be that Bill should do his studying as soon after English class as possible. But from a practical point of view it is difficult to suggest precisely how this can be done for a number of reasons: 1] Each secondary school has a different way of scheduling classes; 2] High School schedules are usually planned very tightly, and students have very little free time during the day; 3] Each parent seems to want his child to study at night, "like I had to do."

Why all the fuss about
when to study? How does this help?

If you find out about how fast (slowly) we learn and how fast we forget, you will have the answer to that question. Look at Figure 2.

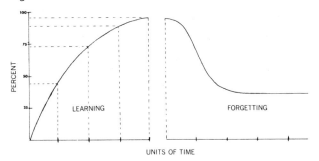

FIG. 2 *Generalized curves of learning and forgetting.*

Notice that when you first begin to work you learn a lot rather quickly; then you begin to slow down. Notice how much you learn in the first unit of time, and how much in the second unit of time. Now, notice how you slow down in the third, fourth, and fifth units. As an illustration, how many times (late at night) have you tried to finish a long unit of study, only to find that near the end of the assignment you are reading the same thing over and over? At that point you have just about stopped learning, and you are wasting time because in the morning probably you could do in ten or fifteen minutes what it would take you an hour to accomplish when you are so tired.

Now comes an even more disappointing part. As soon as we stop learning — in fact, even while we are learning — we begin to forget. If you will look again at Figure 2 you will see that the forgetting part of the curve looks like a sliding board. Down you go, forgetting quickly at first; then you level off. But notice you do level off, and forgetting just about stops. So, for all practical purposes, after twenty-four hours what we still retain (remember) of our original learning we do not forget. The professor would tell us this is a well-known psychological principle: *the longer we know something the less chance we have of forgetting it.*

Here is a classical example of forgetting. Joe Zimmerman, a student mentioned earlier, had an excellent mathematics teacher who was a whiz at explaining algebra problems. Each day when Joe left class he was sure he knew how to do the next day's assignment, but each night when he attempted to work the problems he was stumped. It took him hours to figure them out. Joe asked, "Am I stupid or something? I thought I knew this stuff!" What do you think was wrong with Joe?

Perhaps you have had the same problem — most students have at one time or another. Many students, when asked what they thought was wrong with Joe, stated that he did *not* understand the work. They were wrong. Look back at Figure 2 and you will see the answer. Joe *forgot*. He forgot just enough so that he could not work the problems. He had to go back and relearn. This relearning process took almost as much time as Joe had spent in class. How could Joe (or you) keep from getting on that forgetting sliding board after he (you) learned the algebra in class or memorized THE WRECK OF THE HESPERUS?

First and foremost, a student has to schedule his time. (This discussion will take up only the *when* to learn. Later, in Chapter 3, you will be shown *how* to retain what you have learned.) But any old schedule is not the answer. Joe had a schedule, but it did not help him. Here again the professor came to the rescue with his bit about *the longer we know something.* . . . So, the first step for Joe was to do his math homework *immediately* after class. This was possible three days of the week, but not on the other two days. On the two days when Joe could not study immediately after class we had to him review briefly what he had just learned *so he would not forget.* Then we had him do his math *as soon after class as possible.* Outcome? Believe it or not, this simple suggestion cut in half the amount of time Joe had to spend on his algebra. And, by the way, he did get better grades.

This is only one specific example. What is the general principle involved? Taking all things into consideration, the ideal set-up would be for you to study immediately before classes in which you recite, and immediately after a lecture or demonstration class. The logic of this suggestion becomes clear if you will remember that we want to know the material we have just learned for as long as possible. If we study *before* a question-answer class, that class constitutes a "free" review; consequently, we know and think about the material for a longer period of time. In the case of a lecture class, the teacher does the work (that is, we are shown or told, and we learn without much effort). If you study right after a lecture class you will know (keep) the material you have just learned for a longer period of time. But even more important, in both cases you will be *using* and *applying* what you have just learned. The importance of this fact will become more evident as we discuss *how* to study and how to take tests and examinations.

Now let us get down to some general suggestions on how to

set up a schedule. But please understand that these suggestions will have to be general ones. The author has examined
the schedules of hundreds of students from a great variety of
high schools, and finds it is impossible to tell a person *precisely*
when he should study. You will have to devise your own
schedule, keeping three main facts in mind: 1] Where possible, try to do your most difficult assignments as early in the
day as possible; 2] Study immediately before a class in which
you will be asked questions; 3] Study immediately after a
lecture or demonstration (e.g., mathematics) class.

♦ HERE ARE A FEW MORE SUGGESTIONS to take into considera-
ation before you begin to set up your schedule:

1] It is most important to set up a *workable* schedule which
will fit your needs. No one will have exactly the same activities
as you have, and no one will spend exactly the same amount
of time you spend on a given subject. Therefore, copying or
trying to use another person's schedule just will not work.

2] In setting up a schedule be honest with yourself. Schedule
all the things you have to do, such as going to classes, etc.;
also, schedule those things you know you are going to do,
such as dating, watching television, etc. Do not kid yourself
by scheduling study time when you know you are going to be
doing, or even *want* to be doing, something else.

3] Try to decide just about how much time *you* will need
to do justice to each subject. When we discussed this point
with our high school friends they suggested that we mention
extra work. We found that many high school teachers require
that notebooks be turned in every three or four weeks; others
require a summary report or theme every week or so. Learn in
the beginning to "case" your teachers; find out from the older
students just how much extra work is required, and then plan
a time for it in your schedule.

4] Use your odd hours, half hours, and ten-minute breaks for
studying. You will be as amazed as Joe was at how much you
can accomplish in these short periods. Short study periods are

especially good if you have them early in the day. You are probably fifty percent more efficient in the mornings than you are in the evenings. This means that an hour of study in the morning is usually worth an hour and a half to two hours of study in the evening. In addition, the more work you do during the day the more time you will have in the evening for leisure, hobbies, and for extra assignments. Of course, we know that many parents will object if you do not study at night. It will be up to you to show them *when* you do your work, and prove your point by getting better grades. There are at least three big reasons why you should try to convince your parents that you should try this system: 1] You will learn more and get better grades with less effort;   2] You will have more time for yourself;   3] When your parents find that you are learning how to get things done for yourself and how to use your time, they will (most likely) feel that you deserve a little more freedom in handling your affairs.

5] *By all means, allow for reviews each week.*

6] Since recreational activities will vary from week to week, keep an eye on your schedule and change it to suit your needs. The main idea is that the schedule should be set up so that you can get everything done. Then, if some unexpected event turns up change your schedule so that you borrow time; do not steal it!

7] Use good sense in setting up your schedule and your work place. In the past, some students have gone overboard on planning their time and in selecting a place to study. A schedule then becomes the master, rather than a servant. There is one actual case of a student who spent so much time shopping for and selecting exactly the right study desk and lamp that met all the lighting engineers' specifications that he had no time to study. He had a beautiful study, but he failed all of his courses! Remember, the study environment should be simple and uncluttered, and your time schedule should be usable and workable. Keep it simple.

Specifically, how do you set up a schedule?

1] Make a schedule of how you *think* you spend your time. Use the form provided on page 25. Use different colored pencils for different activities, e.g., blue for recreation, red for "musts" like classes, etc., and green for study time. This system will give you an immediate visual check on the proportion of time you spend in each kind of activity.

2] Keep track of your activities for two weeks to get an idea of how and where you actually spend your time. This idea is particularly important for the student who engages in a great many or a great variety of activities. This student may be surprised to find that when he lists all of his activities there are not enough hours in the day to do everything. Maybe *you* cannot schedule *all* of your activities. Look at your other time-consumers; for example, the time you spend talking to friends in the halls at school or the extra ten minutes at the soda fountain. Did you realize how much time you spent in activities which really did you no good or from which you got very little satisfaction? Would it be better to continue those activities or to use some of that time for study purposes? If you can fit your studies into these times, you will have more time available after school or in the evenings for recreation.

3] After you have recorded your activities for two weeks, compare this schedule with the one you prepared on how you *thought* you spent your time.

4] Make up a schedule for how you *should* spend your time, taking into consideration what you *have* to do, what you *really* want to do, and study time.

5] Keep checking your schedule and revise it as new needs arise. Remember, this schedule is to help you make better use of your time, so use it sensibly. Do not become a slave to the schedule, but also do not make a schedule merely to complete an assignment, and then forget about it. A usable schedule should be flexible enough to allow you time for activities which pop up unexpectedly.

Record of study, classes, and recreation
for a typical high school week

(Sample sheet — make up additional sheets as needed)

	Monday	Tuesday	Wednesday	Thursday	Friday	Saturday	Sunday
7:00							
8:00							
9:00							
10:00							
11:00							
12:00							
1:00							
2:00							
3:00							
4:00							
5:00							
6:00							
7:00							
8:00							
9:00							
10:00							
11:00							

CHAPTER 3

Notemaking

What are your opinions
on the importance of making notes?

By answering the following true or false statements before you
read this chapter you can discover if you agree with those individuals who have studied the topic of notemaking.

1] Notemaking will become a lost art now that we have
   pocket-sized electronic recorders.

2] Notemaking is important only or primarily for students.

3] Most students know how to make good notes, even
   though they do not use them.

4] One cannot listen and write at the same time.

5] Taking notes in class slows down learning.

6] Most students do not know *why* they should make notes.

7] There is no difference between note*making* and note-
   taking.

8] Brilliant and/or successful people do not ordinarily use
   crutches such as notes.

9] If it is necessary to make notes, one should copy what
   was said or read as exactly as time permits.

10] One-word outlines are a good way to make notes, if notes
    are necessary.

How did you respond? Only number 6 should have been marked *true*; all others are definitely false.

Just who besides students makes notes, and what purpose do notes serve?

"Good morning, J. D. I hope you have recovered from that stomach trouble." (A few more words of greeting.) "By the way, how is your son doing at Northwestern? Last time I heard he had almost a "B" average . . ."

Mr. Alfred Perident, a salesman for a large manufacturing company, usually greets his customers with this kind of personal greeting. At least part of his $50,000 plus a year salary is due to the fact that he seldom, if ever, makes a mistake, knows his customers intimately, and never bores them. It is also claimed that he is an excellent story-teller, and has the reputation for never telling a customer the same story twice.

How can Mr. Perident keep all of his customers, their children, and his stories straight, and how is it he does not make mistakes? The author asked Mr. Perident the same question. "The answer," he said, "is simple. I make notes." Whereupon he showed the author his card-file notebook. Each customer was listed on a card, and each card contained all kinds of personal information about family, hobbies, and jokes, and a brief summary of the previous conversation, plus a special section for questions the customer asked.

Is Mr. Perident unusual, or do other successful people make notes, too? If you have watched any of the so-called public service programs, detective stories, or round-table discussions on television, you know the answer to that question. If you have seen a telecast of the United Nations meetings you have probably observed the delegates writing notes on the little pads before them. Why should this be necessary when there are so many stenographers and electrical gadgets recording the conferences? Well, suppose the delegate from Outer Mongolia wants to question a precise point made by Madame Delegate from Djibouti. Can he gracefully interrupt the conference by turning back one of the recorders or have a secretary read from her notebook? Then, too, you have probably noticed your favorite television detective making notes on conversations. These people make notes on what is said so they will have important comments, ideas, and information available when they want them, and ready for immediate reference.

Notes serve many other useful purposes, as we shall see as we progress through this chapter. Of course, you may not figure on becoming a $50,000 a year salesman or a United Nations delegate, but there are other purposes for notes. Good note-making habits will be valuable if only to keep you from forgetting anniversaries or what you are supposed to say at the next meeting of your favorite chowder and marching society.

Why is it that high school students do not make notes?

They do, in some cases. But when the author talked with high school students he discovered that although they did in many cases takes notes, they were quite dissatisfied with the results. The students sang a variety of blues: "I just never got into the habit of noting things I want to remember; it takes too long; I put the stuff down, but it just isn't right; *I can't pay attention and write at the same time.*" Although these are just a few of the comments, they do show the crux of the difficulty. Most people try to *take* notes, rather than *make* notes. But even more basic is the fact that students do not know *why* or *how* to make notes.

Why is notemaking important, and how can it help me?

First, let us take a look at why notemaking is important. Many of us believe that we can learn by being exposed to knowledge or information, and that we can absorb learning in the same way we pick up a sun tan. This is far from the truth. In order to learn we must work at learning, and in order to work we must be active. We must be actively interested in what is being said or done, and we must *do something* to learn. Sitting in a class merely listening or merely reading a book are not examples of being active. When we listen or read without doing anything else (e.g., checking on what we have heard or read) we do not really know whether we have learned anything. Suppose you are told that *ontogeny recapitulates phylogeny.* Certainly you heard, but did you learn anything? Our friend the professor would tell us that there are two problems involved (and he could prove there are, too): 1] We forget much of what we have learned within a few hours (see Figure 2, p. 19; 2] Much of what we think we have forgotten we never really learned in the first place.

Now to complete answering the questions asked at the beginning of this section. Making a set of good notes will help you to keep your mind from wandering and force you to pay close attention. When you are able to write down what you have heard, you know that you have learned the material to which you have been exposed. In addition, your forgetting will be greatly slowed down.

To explain further why you should make notes let us begin by saying that the greatest benefit to be derived from a set of good notes comes *during* the process of making them. First of all, one has to pay very close attention in order to be able to make good notes. Paying close attention, digesting the material, and writing notes is a form of activity which will help, if not assure, that you will absorb more of the information (you have just digested) than you would absorb if you had merely listened. Having made notes you can find out how much you really did learn, and how well you understood what was said or read. In addition, this activity will pay off in other ways. Having learned more initially, you will have less reviewing to do at examination time; and when you do review, all of the material will be in one place, which means more time saved.

How does good notemaking
slow down forgetting?

As we said before, much of what we think we have forgotten we never really knew in the first place. Notemaking gives us an immediate check on what we have or have not learned.

More important, however, is the fact that in order to write notes we must first listen *attentively*, go over the material in our heads, then write the notes. In other words, we have gone over the material at least twice after we heard or learned it. These repetitions are very similar to what we do when we learn a song: we hear it, repeat it several times, and then we know it. But we do not stop there. We sing the song quite a few more times before we tire of it. By that time we have *overlearned* the song, and the chances are we just *will not forget it*. If we apply that same principle to learning what was said in class, what questions the teacher asked, and what we read in our textbooks, we *can* learn our school work almost as easily as we learn a song. And, like the song, we will not forget it.

Build a new skill on the foundation of what you already know.

Suppose at this point you are convinced that there is a good reason for making notes, but you bring up the most frequently raised objection: "I can't pay attention and take notes at the same time." We have already explained that one can pay attention better if one makes notes. But before we explain the mechanics of notemaking for *study* purposes, let us look at an everyday example of notemaking reduced to its bare essentials and see what you already know about notemaking. Your mother says:

> Ferdinand, I'd like you to go downtown this afternoon and pick up a few things for me. (At this point you would get a pencil and paper to make notes on what your mother is going to ask you to do. Your mother continues.) Go into the Sewing Center and get a spool of #30, white, mercerized, cotton thread. Oh, and while you are there get a pack of left-handed needles. Now be sure to get them at the Sewing Center because they cost less there. I'd also like you to get three, four-ounce, medium bottles. The 5 & 10 is the only place where they are sold. And you might as well pick up my dress at the "Bon Ton" while you're down there. You

can get yourself that do-it-yourself atomic bomb kit I promised you. On your way home pick up a cherry pie for dinner
from the bakery shop right near the bus stop.

When your mother has finished giving you the instructions
you would probably have a list (notes!) like this:

sewing center—1 #30, white, mercerized cotton
              1 set left-handed needles
5 & 10—3 4 oz. med. bottles
Bon Ton—mother's dress
bakery shop—cherry pie

You now plan your stops downtown according to the most
convenient route, and list the items to be taken care of at each
stop. You have put down what *you need to know*. The atomic
bomb kit was omitted because you probably will not have to
be reminded that you want it. The chances are that once you
are downtown you will be able to recall some of the items
without looking at the list. You may, for example, recall that
you want thread and needles, but what about the #30, mercerized, and left-handed part! Suppose you were told to get
ten items and (without your list) forgot four of them; on a
test your score would be 60. "Oh, ho," you say, "but you can't
use notes on a test." True, but at this point we are only
beginning our process of learning. In the next chapter you will
learn more about how to study your material so you can use a
list on examinations — and legally, too. In fact, if you study
correctly you have a good list to take into examinations, but
the list will be in your head where you can really use it, and
use it *conveniently*.

Let us go back to our example. If we are to make notes we
must know the purpose of the notes and how they are to be
used. Let us suppose that on the day you were downtown getting the items for your mother someone broke into the chemistry teacher's offices and "borrowed" the school's supply of
uranium. Time of theft was between 3 P.M. and 4 P.M. As
one of the students interested in atomic bomb kits, you are a
suspect. A local detective questions you as to your where-

abouts, and you tell him about your trip downtown. His notes might look like this:

> Suspect states he boarded bus at 1:05 P.M., arrived downtown at 1:35. Proceeded to sewing center — arrived approx. 1:40, left 2:10. Uncertain about time at 5 & 10, but is sure he was at Bon Ton at 2:45, and at hobby shop at 3:15. Boarded bus for home at 3:40, bakery shop 4:30. Arrived home 4:50.

It is quite simple to see that there are great differences between both the *form* and *content* of your notes for the trip downtown and the detective's notes. You will notice that the detective's notes do *not* contain the articles you bought. What was his purpose in making notes? He was not interested in what you bought; he was interested in what you were doing when the theft occurred. You will also notice that he used complete thoughts in the form of (more or less) complete sentences. Why the difference? Simply this: for *his* purpose this form of notemaking is better than making a list. Your words and complete statements are important to him. He wants, as any good detective would say, *all the facts.*

How can you apply what you already know about notemaking to your school work? The trouble is that many people who talk about *taking* notes either complicate the process or worry too much about oversimplifying it. They emphasize oversimplified outlining, underlining, and similar devices. The oversimplified outline (consisting only of one or two words to remind a person of a whole paragraph or page) may be fine for some people (e.g., when they are thoroughly familiar with the material, and need only to be reminded of a sequence). On the other hand, outlining is sometimes elaborate. But is the fussing with Roman numerals (I), capital letters (A), Arabic numerals (1), small letters and numbers (a, ii), etc., really worth the time it takes! Besides, only a real brain can keep track of which letter or number to put down and which comes next when he is trying to get a series of facts on paper.

In order to make meaningful notes it is necessary to start out by getting facts down in *your own words.* If this is really the case, the other oversimplified "notemaking" system (underlining) is the greatest hoax of all. If you are not allowed to mark up your books, wonderful! Actually, underlining is good practice for only one thing — drawing lines. In class and on tests you answer questions and/or recite. So, in *all* your studying, begin by practicing the reaction you will use later, i.e., answering questions in your own words.

In learning *how* to make a set of good notes students seem to need only a few guiding principles in order to get themselves started. With that thought in mind we are going to suggest only one method for making notes, a method which was devised after much experimentation and study, and which was found to be simple and applicable to just about every situation and requirement.[1] We call our method the S.O.S. system of notemaking (*Summarize, Organize, Systematize*) which we believe will help to Save Our Students. But please consider that the S.O.S. system is a *skill*, and you will have to practice it with the idea of improving if you want to become proficient. Learn the *basic* idea of this system, and you will find you can use it for classroom or textbook notemaking, and that it will be as applicable for your every day notemaking needs as for the class where the instructor requires that you turn in an elaborate notebook.

❨ *Summarize (in class).*

The main idea in all summarizing is to write *enough* to remind you of what was said. In the two going-downtown examples given, we had a list and a series of sentences. In some cases you will need just a list (e.g., when your teacher tells you to "look up the definitions of the following words . . ."), and in other cases you may need a complete sentence (e.g., when your teacher says, "*it is important for you to know* that the turning point in this battle occurred when the French artillery units failed to begin firing on the British flank positions at the prescribed time.")

[1] For students who become interested in additional notemaking systems, see George Weigand and Walter S. Blake. (24, pp. 30-34).

In some classes the teachers will ask quite a few questions. Write these questions in your notebook. Now, listen to the answer or answers given, and pay attention to the teacher's reactions and statements. Does he change or add anything to the answers given by the students? When you have the *complete* answer, *condense* that answer mentally, put it into your own words, and write it in your notebook. In another class the teacher may begin to lecture (our high school spies tell us that this method is becoming increasingly popular in some secondary schools). When he does, follow the same procedure. First, listen carefully until the teacher makes a complete statement, or gives a complete thought or idea. Is that statement important enough to remember, or is it just explanatory or illustrative material? Notice that you have to pay attention to the point where you can decide which statements are important and which are merely illustrative. Suppose you decide the statement is important. Condense the thought or idea (*in your own words*) and write it in your notebook. Again, notice that not only have you gone over the material to decide whether it is important, but you have condensed it, put it into your own words, and written it in your notebook — all in the space of a few seconds (that is, after you have practiced for a while). All this means that you have been over what was said several times; you have already begun to overlearn. But please remember that the Secret of Success of the S.O.S. method lies in just five words: *summarize in your own words*.

There are two main objections sometimes raised to this system. First, it takes too much time. But does it? At first you *will* take additional time, but with a little practice you will find it very easy and quite quick. Second, many students say, "I can't write and listen at the same time." True, but only if you try to *copy* the teacher's words. If you understand the thought and put it into your own words, you can write what you know and listen at the same time. Again, *practice* is necessary for proficiency.

There is another big reason for suggesting this method. It is usually impossible and/or worthless to write down exactly what the teacher said (unless, of course, he *wants* you to copy a definition or passage; then he will tell you and/or talk slowly enough so you can copy his words). First of all, you cannot write fast enough to copy his every word, and even if you could you would be wasting time. There are reasons for the last statement: 1] you *do not* need everything that is said; you *do* need *facts*; 2] anyone can parrot words and phrases, but you will have to *understand* what is said in order to put ideas down in your own words; 3] later on you will have to use your own words on tests and examinations, so why not start practicing now! As you practice this procedure you will begin to understand, first, in all notemaking it is necessary to get facts, and second, that the *greatest* benefit from a good set of notes comes in the process of making them.

❲ *Summarize (from the textbook)* .

First, read a section of your textbook. How large a section? This is difficult to say. The size of the section is entirely up to you and your background and ability in a given subject. You may read a section, a page, or just a paragraph. The guiding principle here it to read as large a *logical* section as you can without losing your train of thought. Now, STOP! How much of the section can you recall? What did it say? (After you study the next chapter of this book where you are taught how to make up questions before you read a section, you can try to answer the questions you have made up on each section.) If you know what the section said, and can answer your own questions, write down a brief summary (*again, in your own words*) of the section. If after reading you have difficulty recalling all the points, use a shorter section for your next reading. With practice you will be able to judge just how large a section you should read (in each text) before you review and write down your summary. As you progress to the next section of this book (on how to study a prose-type textbook) you will find additional hints which will help you to revise this system of notemaking so it will be most helpful for *you*.

⟮ *Organize.*

How to organize what you have summarized can be shown by taking our going-downtown example. Suppose, after noting what your mother asked you to get, you rearranged the list of stores so you could go down the street on one side visiting stores, and up the other side and back to the bus terminal. In other words, you could save quite a bit of time by organizing your visits so that you could avoid backtracking, jay-walking, etc.

If the material presented by your teacher and/or the textbook was well organized your summary notes constitute a well-organized set of notes. If your teacher insists on an outline, you *have* an outline; only the letters and numbers are missing. On the other hand, if the material was disorganized, mixed up, or jumbled, rearrange the facts so your notes will be in a logical sequence. This logical sequence of facts should give a *complete idea* of what was presented in each class and/or in each section of the textbook.

⟮ *Systematize.*

We have suggested that you make notes on your textbook readings and on the material your teacher gives in class. In some subjects you may also be expected to do outside reading and/or required to turn in a set of notes on this reading. At this point you may have two or three well-organized summaries, but you do not have one complete, logical summary of the topic being studied. The serious student who wants to learn should systematize his notes by combining all summaries into one complete story on each topic covered in class.

There is one further step which can and should be taken to get the most from your notes. List *all* the questions you have (those you have made up, those your teacher asked, those you have heard from your friends, etc.) in the margin of your pages of notes — opposite the answer in your notes. In order to do this you should set up your notes so that this can be done.

Possibly you might start by using a notebook which is already set up to help you to organize and to systematize your notes. After your notes have been organized and systematized you can conduct a very quick review by answering the questions you have listed. If you miss a question you can find the answer in your own notes without further searching.

If your teacher is the type who demands that you turn in a nice, neat, well-organized notebook once a week or once a month, this notemaking system is made to order for you. In the "Summarize" state you have gathered all the necessary information. Often, at this point, students merely recopy their notes in a more *legible fashion*. This procedure is a waste of time (see end of this chapter for an explanation). If your teacher requires that you hand in a notebook, make this assignment a form of study. *Organize* and *systematize* your notes and get some real benefit from the assignment. Actually, this kind of reorganization of notes should be carried out whether or not your teacher requires this type of notebook because it is one of the best forms of reviewing. And finally, be sure to do your reorganizing in each course at least once a week. The size of the task of several weeks' review and reorganization will discourage you. But there is still a better reason — if you really review each week you will not have to worry about those *frantic* reviews before tests and examinations.

A few hints on notemaking.

To be perfectly honest with you, no one can tell you *exactly* how to make notes. All of us who are interested can make suggestions on which procedures are best and on how to improve your technique, but there is absolutely no substitute for practice!

◆ HERE ARE A FEW HINTS which will help you to get started right.

1] Make up your mind right now that you are going to make notes even though at this point you are not convinced that you need them. Try making notes for a few weeks, and let the *results* convince you either to continue or to give up the idea. Keep trying to improve your notemaking procedures.

2] Be sure to get seated in class a few minutes before the bell rings. Get yourself into the swing of things by reading over both yesterday's classroom notes and your textbook notes on today's assignment. Incidentally, this is an excellent form of study, and will cut down appreciably on the time it takes you to review for a test.

3] Use a *large*, three-ring notebook, preferably one which takes 8½" x 11" sheets. With this type of notebook you will have more room, and will make more and better notes. Also, this type of notebook allows you to arrange your notes and to include any syllabi or mimeographed sheets your teacher might give to you. There are two other things you should consider here. First, use *only one* notebook. Those students who use several notebooks often find they have taken the wrong one home or brought the wrong one to class. Second, do *not* use a clip or clamp board. It is too easy to lose or damage the sheets of paper.

4] Number your pages according to the course (e.g., P.O.D. 15) and put the date at the top of each page. This will save you from committing mayhem if your younger brother or sister should accidentally disarrange all of your notes.

5] Now to make your notes. Start with a pen, since penciled notes become smudged, smeared, and unusable after a short while. Next, do more listening than writing. Be sure you have a *complete* thought or idea; summarize it in your head, and then write it down in your own words. But *how* do you listen? Watch and listen for: *a*] what the teacher emphasizes; *b*] the things which are repeated; *c*] *all* questions having to do with the subject matter; *d*] items written on the black (green) board. Consider this one fact: a teacher can think of only so many questions. If you write down *all* questions, you probably will have a copy of the final examination before the teacher writes it!

You should also learn to recognize your teacher's idiosyncracies [this is known as casing the old girl (man)]. Some teachers give a sly smile when they think of a real sneaky question, while others stomp on the floor or pound the desk. There is also the teacher who pauses dramatically and displays his profile while you drink in the wisdom of his words. Every good teacher is at least fifty percent actor, so learn early to recognize when he puts on which act.

In addition to these "give aways" there are statements which will tell you what or how many notes you should have.

A] *Introductory Statements*
  1) The four main causes . . . . (*get four*).
  2) Many reasons have been given . . . . (*how many?*)
  3) The important results of . . . . (*how many and what were those results? Also, were there any minor results?*)
  4) This topic is important because . . . . (*why?*)
B] *Evaluative Statements*
  1) Here is a good definition of —————.
  2) Most experts would agree that —————.
  3) I feel that this is important because —————.

6] Use only one side (the right side of your notebook) of the page for notemaking. The left side of the page can then be used for additions to or corrections for the notes. Some students, however, prefer to use the right-hand pages for class notes and the left-hand pages for textbook notes. Those students say that it is handy for them to have what the teacher said and what the text said in the same place, and that using both sides of the page also helps very much in cutting down on the time spent when they organize and systematize. These are only suggestions. But try these systems, and select the one most suited to your needs.

7] After you have practiced making notes for about a week, compare your notes with those of other students. Also, check with your teachers and see if you cannot get a few suggestions on how to improve.

FINAL NOTE. Notes are for *your* use. Make notes in a usable form, and do not waste time merely recopying them. If your teacher insists that you turn in your notebook, and you have to improve the looks of things, *reorganize* your notes. Make this reorganization serve as a good form of study and review. As we said before, just recopying is a waste of time. When the average person copies he is so intent on not missing a word and on being neat that he is unable to put any time on learning the facts in the notes. On the other hand, when you organize and systematize, you spend approximately the same amount of time as in recopying, but you have to think and work at using the material in a different way. Your material is now *reorganized* into meaningful sections, and your summaries are connected with a great many questions. This means that you are getting *all* your material lined up so that you will be able to use what you have learned.

Finally, you will find that in a very short time your courses will seem much easier, but, more important, you will be learning more. Please do not get the idea that college is the only place where you will be able to apply your notemaking skill after you get out of high school. Notemaking is a skill you can use in any job or business which requires that you have a high school education.

CHAPTER **4**

Mend Your Study Habits

Some time ago, Philip Knowell, a friend of the author, purchased a Hammond electric organ. Philip's ten year old son was fascinated by the instrument, and soon taught himself to play a few tunes. Phil, who is a musician, was encouraged by an obvious display of musical talent. He approached his son about taking organ lessons. "Why should I take lessons?" asked the son. "I can play well enough right now." Phil's son still plays simple tunes quite well, but he has not improved much over a two-year period. An obvious waste of talent! Yet, this is the story of thousands upon thousands of high school students; they have never learned (or have never been taught) how to use many of their basic abilities.

If you decided that you wanted to learn how to play the piano, or wanted to become captain of the football team, what would you do?

The chances are that if you wanted to learn a skill (piano, football, sewing) you would realize that you need a teacher or coach. And you would practice under the direction of that coach or teacher; that is, you would *participate actively* in the development of a skill. Suppose on the other hand you decided you wanted to be able to use what you are learning in your school subjects, or you decided you wanted to get good grades. What would you do? How would you go about changing your study habits so you *would* learn more? Or, if you are already getting good grades, how can you learn more in less time?

How would you solve this problem?

Janice has done an outstanding job working as a part-time typist for a well-known author of historical novels. The author has told Janice that when she graduates from high school next year the job of personal secretary is hers if she fulfills three conditions: 1]improves her English and gets an "A" for her senior English course; 2] gets an "A" in one year of American history; 3] learns enough about doing reference work in history so she can be of assistance in checking historical facts contained in the writer's novels.

List the suggestions on how to study you would give to Janice to assure her getting "A's" in the two courses mentioned.

What is the problem here? Don't most students know how to study if they really put their minds to it?

The answer is an emphatic NO! Most students suggest *reading* and *rereading* the assignments and listening attentively in class. But why do most students think they can master their studies merely by reading and listening? The answer is (as we have said before) simply because they have not been *taught* (many have been told) what *studying* is and how to go about studying. This statement is supported by the fact that one of the complaints most frequently mentioned by students in Agatha Townsend's book, COLLEGE FRESHMEN SPEAK OUT (23), is that they were *never taught how to study and how to apply what they had learned.*

Contrary to what you may think, efficient study is a skill, and not a characteristic or ability given to us by the Almighty; and since efficient study is a skill, *it can be developed.* Just reading an assignment is like watching a game: you may be able to follow the action of a game (by watching), but you will never be able to play it until you get out and practice and actively participate in it. Yet, students just *read* their assignments. "Well," you say, "who is to blame for this? When we get an assignment we are told to *read* it." True, but unfortunately this is one very good reason why so few students know how to study effectively. We hope to remedy that.

Why do you learn and recall
some things easily but not others?

Let us begin to build a skill on a foundation of what you already know. And, let us start by looking at some of the things you already know about yourself, particularly in reference to how you learn and forget. First of all, we do not forget what we have *really learned,* but we often cannot recall (remember) some fact when we are asked to do so. Have you had an experience similar to this one?

> Alan and some friends were sitting around having a soda and talking about last year's big dance. One of his friends asked, "Al, who is the fellow who showed up at the dance last year and had all the girls following him? You know, the character who wore a yellow cummerbund . . . You should know, Al, you were really unhappy about it!" Al hemmed and hawed for a few minutes, trying to recall the name. Finally he gave up. Later that evening, while watching one of his favorite television programs, the name came to him: Sol O'Mara. "That's the name, Sol O'Mara."

In the preceding example had Alan forgotten the name? Hardly, but he could not recall it when asked to do so. You may not see how this example applies to studying unless you recall a similar incident which *must* have happened to you.

> You are taking a history test and you come across the question: What famous battle of the Revolution, George Washington's first real victory, took only forty-five minutes from start to finish? No response. You try and try, but no answer comes to you. Later while talking with some friends, you suddenly recall: Christmas Eve — The Battle of Trenton. But the answer does not do you very much good at that time.

Many additional examples could be given, but just one more should suffice.

Why is it when you memorize two "poems" of roughly

equal length you are able to recall one, but can make only a feeble attempt at recalling the other? Suppose your teacher tells you to memorize Portia's famous quality-of-mercy speech. At the same time you and your current "steady" hear a tune on the juke box which you decide will be "our song." A year later (or even twenty years later) you can still sing that song, but the quality of mercy is quite a strain. Why is it you are able to sing the song, but make only a feeble attempt at reciting the speech? Suppose you could master the speech and other materials from your school courses and keep them for future reference, and without any more real effort than it took to learn the song! Well, cheer up; it can be done.

Why should there be such a difference in ability to recall? First, there is a big difference both in the way you learned and in the reason for learning the poem and the song. *You* wanted to learn the song; the *teacher* wanted you to learn the poem. The author constantly encounters students who can give a list of the best selling songs for the past ten years, the performance figures for all popular automobiles or sports cars, and/or complete data on which actors and actresses have been married to whom and how many times. Yet many of these same students say they "can't memorize poems" or "can't memorize formulas and dates of historical events." Think about it for a minute. Does it make sense that the same person who can recite all the facts about cars, songs, and actresses cannot learn formulas and dates and events from a history book?

Why do you learn?

Up to this point you can see that each of us does learn. In the meantime, quite a bit has been said here about *how* you learn, although you may not recognize this fact at the moment. Now, let us turn to why you learn. Again, have you had this experience?

You sit down at the telephone table, look up a number in the telephone directory, dial the number, and then put the directory away as you hear the first ring. But then a voice interrupts with, "What number are you calling, please?" You did not expect this. You hesitate, then admit you do not recall the number you just dialed.

Just about everyone has had this or a similar experience, but why does it happen? The answer is very simple. You looked up the number only to *dial* it, not to *learn* and *remember* it. After you dialed the number you had no further use for it — you *thought!*

We can find another example of difference in ability to recall if we look at you as you studied for that last test. The chances are you crammed. That is, you did all of your work at one time, and although the method was effective for a *short period of time*, you "forgot" the material after the test. Why was the cramming method effective for a short period of time? Because when you studied for the test you probably feverishly repeated (recited) facts, figures, answers, etc., over and over again. Yes, you probably *read* the facts, but you recited them over and over again. But what happened after the test? You promptly "forgot" what you had learned. And when the teacher announced another test on the same material you had to go back and relearn all of the material you had already "learned" before. *What a waste of time!* With just a little more effort (hardly noticeable) all of this relearning would be unnecessary.

Can you figure out why you can recall certain facts and forget others so soon?

Our old friend the professor could have told you this is what would happen, and he could have gone on to tell you why. He could tell you that way back in the 1800's a man named Ebbinghaus spent more time and effort studying memory than you spend on recreation! Ebbinghaus made some startling discoveries about memory, and was able to explain scientifically what *you* know about memory. First of all, he could tell you we forget much of what we have learned very soon after we learn it, and he could show you this graph: (see Figure 2, p. 19). In addition, this graph should indicate that the more you learn at one time (cram) the more you forget (soon after you have learned).

The professor would then tell you about some of Ebbinghaus's other experiments which explain why you can sing the old song or recall the telephone number of some "ex" long after it is of any use to you. He would say you *overlearned* the song and telephone number. *Overlearning* occurs when a fact is learned, and then repeated and repeated until it becomes fixed in a person's mind. Perhaps overlearning can be compared with scratching a diagram in very hard ground with a stick: the more you go over the outline of the diagram, the clearer it becomes. A good example of this is your name. Even if you were marooned on a desert island and did not hear your name spoken or referred to again, sixty years later, when you were rescued, you could still recall it with no effort. Ebbinghaus's experiments showed that the more you overlearn a given fact (sing that song, dial that number) the less chance there is that you will forget it.

How can these facts be applied
in helping you to study more efficiently?

First, use the same technique for learning your daily assignments as you used in studying for that test or learning that song — *recite* and *recite* over again. Space your learning, as was suggested in the chapter on schedules. *Do not cram* or try to learn everything at one time. Then protect the investment in time and effort you expended in your original learning by reviewing at least once a week. This last suggestion will help you to avoid two things: 1] not being able to recall the answer to a test question when you want it, and 2] forgetting what you have learned as soon as the test is finished.

At this point we expect strong objections. Students are not convinced that they should change their work habits because *studying* takes more time than just reading. Of course it does—at first. But later on, after you have become accustomed to the methods suggested here, you will find that planning your time and using efficient study techniques *will save you time in the long run.* In fact, if you study efficiently you will spend less time and get more, much more, out of your school work and, incidentally, get better grades than you do now. You will spend less time and learn more because when you use the techniques which are suggested you will read faster, and when you overlearn, you learn for keeps. Result, there will be no more frantic reviewing and no more all-night cramming sessions. Sure, you will have to spend a *little* extra time now to save a *lot* of time later.

What are the suggestions
for quicker and easier learning?

Most students do want to keep permanently what they learn when they find out how they can accomplish this in a relatively painless way. But you must want to learn before any of these suggestions will be effective for you. Please forget about systems you might have learned from friends, parents, or even from the mathematical genius who lives next door. Whereas some systems are fair, most popular systems are downright idiotic. Many experimenters have worked on the problem of how to learn and have presented a great variety of ideas. Most experimenters, however, emphasize certain points:

1] Time-place habit; that is, have a definite time and a definite place or places for study.

2] Plan ahead to do your work; plan which courses you are going to study; plan how you are going to do each assignment.

3] Keep alert while learning by being active, by doing something. The best type of activity is practicing what you are going to do later. Therefore, ask and answer questions, and make notes.

4] Comprehend the material. Make a definite effort to understand what you are reading while you are reading. Read to answer questions.

5] Check yourself to see if you do understand what you have read. You can do this by reciting what you have learned *without* looking at your book or notes.

6] Protect the investment of time by fixing the material in your memory. At this stage you overlearn by reciting the material in several different ways.

7] Space your learning; do not cram.

8] Review relatively frequently to keep the material at your finger tips so you can recall it when you want or need it. These reviews should be short.

In addition, certain other suggestions are made:

1] Check yourself to be sure you are learning accurately. Check your answers against your source of information.

2] Try for accuracy and mastery at the beginning or elementary phases of the particular course.

3] Try to line up your studies or any other task with something useful. In other words, understand how learning a subject or doing a job is going to help you.

PROBLEM: How can all these points be applied while studying?

Fortunately there are many convenient ways to remember all of these suggestions if you have a schedule, and stick to it. Probably the best known and most widely used formula for study is the "SQ3R" method. "SQ3R" stands for "Survey, Question, Read, Recite, Review." [1] While this method is very effective for college students, the author believes that certain changes and modifications should be made in it for high school use. For high school students the author suggests, SARTOR, a

[1] Robinson (20).

tailor-made method for mending your study habits. These letters stand for "Scan, Ask, Read, Talk (over), Overlearn, and Review." But in order to apply SARTOR a certain amount of explanation is necessary.

1] *Scan the whole assignment.*

If you were going out on a date you would make *some* plans. If you decided on a trip you would have some idea of where you wanted to go and how to get there. But studying! No plans! If you are really going to study you must plan your work. Look over the assignment to see what it is all about. You can do this in one of several ways: look over the topic headings or the list of questions at the end of the chapter; or, read the summary at the end of the chapter, if there is a summary. In the event the author has made *no* attempt to give you any clues as to what he thinks is important, you can always use one of the popular outline books which are available on just about any subject. If you follow *any one* of these suggestions you will have an idea of what is coming and what is important, and you will be very pleased to find out how much faster your reading will be, how much more sense your reading will make, and how much more you will learn.

2] *Ask!*

Ask what? This is a good question, but the answer is up to you. First, ask yourself what *should* you be learning and what do you *want* to learn about the subject. Next, ask yourself about the important points you picked up in your scanning; how can you use this information to make up questions similar to the ones your teacher will ask? Make up as many questions as possible, but try to make up at least one question for each paragraph *before* you read it. These questions will help to keep you alert.

In addition to keeping your attention focused on the big points and keeping you alert, these questions will help in other respects. In the first place, you will use most of what you learn in high school to answer questions in class and on tests. Although studying in the way we suggest will help you to learn your course material so that it will be of value to you in every day life, these questions will help you directly to prepare for classroom recitation and quizzes. In other words, *you are practicing the reaction you will use later,* i.e., answering questions. There is one other point in connection with making up questions. If you make up enough of your own and check with your friends (this point will be discussed later) to find out their questions, your teacher probably will not be able to come up with anything you have not already answered. Think of how you would feel walking into an examination and seeing only questions you have already answered! Enough said?

Perhaps you are one of those persons who wonders why we emphasize questions — answers — examinations — grades. For one very good reason: we are practical. You are going to take examinations and get grades; this is part of the educational system. This system is here to stay, so why not learn what it is and how to beat it, not buck it!

3] *Read—but read to answer your questions.*

What happens when you read? Let us say you are an average person reading a bit of early American history. You are trying to get through a particularly dull account of Indian life. As you come to the end of one line you learn that the Indians' chief means of water transportation was the canoe. Canoe, you repeat to yourself as your eyes go wandering off in space . . . oh, for those days on Lake Oshkosh in my canoe, with Gwendolyn playing her mandolin . . . soft breezes . . . A half hour later you are still on Lake Oshkosh; you have been turning the pages of the book, but all you can recall about the assignment is the blue of Gwendolyn's eyes. What happened? Who can get this stuff anyhow? Well, *you* could if you knew how to read. But at this point what do you do if you have to learn what is in the book? You *reread* the whole chapter. Let us suppose that you had read ten pages before you began to dream of Gwendolyn, and ten pages after you began to dream. How much do you know of those first ten pages? Suppose you have learned 90% of the material on those pages. When you reread, you spend as much time on those first ten pages (which you know) as on the last ten pages (which you do not know). Actually, we are all guilty of both of these faults. If we were not, there would be no need for the explanation which follows on how to do study-type reading.

In study-type reading you should first scan; then ask questions. When you read, keep your questions in mind, and read to answer these questions. Begin by reading a short, logical section. Now, STOP! How much of the section can you recite *without* referring to your book? Can you answer your questions? If not, you did not read carefully enough. Go back and reread only that section you did not understand. When you do understand the section, write a summary of it in your notebook as you learned how to do in the section on note-making. Also, try to make up additional questions *after* reading the section, and write them in your notebook.

If you carry out your reading in this fashion, your first few attempts will take quite a bit of time. But once you establish a *habit*, you will really begin to speed up. Your assignments will take less time because you are forcing yourself to pay attention—no more daydreaming and time-wasting. And in a short while, *studying* your assignment and making notes on it will take no more time than you formerly took *merely* reading.

4] *Talk Over.*

Who ever heard high school students talk over or talk about their school subjects? The author has, and quite frequently, too — at examination time. "What do you think Miss Lawrence will ask about the Whiskey Rebellion? Is it true that the Whiskey Rebellion is the only movement that has no 'sons of'? What was it that Johnson said about the fellow who made George Washington's false teeth — and who did anyhow?

What are you going to study in English?" Why talk over these points with other students, and why wait until examination time? Well, obviously you feel there is some value in asking these questions or you wouldn't do it. But you have waited too long to get any real, lasting value from your efforts.

There are numerous ways you can talk over your lessons. One way is to recite in class. In college courses on effective study methods it is suggested that students recite instead of talk over. This suggestion is made because college students get less chance for class recitation than do high school students. Actually, you have a wonderful oportunity to hear the teacher's questions and your own answers prior to examination time. You may not think of classroom recitation as an advantage, but it is actually an excellent aid in learning. The idea of recitation is not new. Our old friend the professor could point out a great many experiments to show you the value of recitation. In fact, he might show you the following table to point out a number of things.

TABLE I

The value of recitation in memorizing.

(GATES, 1917)

MATERIAL STUDIED	16 NONSENSE SYLLABLES		5 SHORT BIOGRAPHIES, TOTALING ABOUT 170 WORDS	
	PERCENT REMEMBERED		PERCENT REMEMBERED	
	immediately	*after 4 hours*	*immediately*	*after 4 hours*
All time devoted to reading	35	15	35	16
1/5 of time devoted to recitation	50	26	37	19
2/5 of time devoted to recitation	54	28	41	25
3/5 of time devoted to recitation	57	37	42	26
4/5 of time devoted to recitation	74	48	42	26

First, notice how long ago this experiment was made. Also, pay particular attention to the columns under "16 nonsense syllables." *Nonsense material* is simply material which makes no sense to *you*. A good example of nonsense is $C_{12} H_{22} O_{11}$; that is, unless you have studied chemistry and know it is sugar. ἐς κόρακας may be Greek to you, but to a Greek it is "drop dead." However, if you were studying chemistry or Greek and wanted to learn these symbols you would have a better chance of learning them if you recited them frequently until you memorized them. After these symbols are memorized, you can begin to use them in the construction of chemical formulae or Greek sentences. Now these symbols will begin to mean something to you as you learn to use them. Presto! They are no longer memorized nonsense but meaningful formulae and words. So, in all your studying, recite or talk over the material until you have it fixed in your memory. But remember, the *less* meaningful the subject, the more you should recite.

Perhaps tables and graphs do not mean much to you. Possibly you need a practical example. You have probably often wondered why you can recall things you have talked about with your friends much better than you can remember what you have read. Think for a minute. You can read a selection without knowing what you read. It is rather hard to talk about something when you know nothing about it, even though there are a great many people who try to disprove that point! Usually you have to have *some* idea about a topic to talk about it. When you talk about this topic you are going over something you already know, and you are *overlearning* it. And as the professor predicted, you would remember material better if you *overlearned* it. So why not try to talk over your subjects? Overlearn and get the other fellows' ideas on what questions your teacher will ask. Then you not only have your own questions but those of several other people. And even though your teachers may not appreciate this statement in this connection, several heads are better than one, even though one of the several is yours. Together, several of you can outguess your teachers as far as questions are concerned!

5] *Overlearn.*

You have a list of questions from your teacher and from other sources, and you have talked over the answers and recited them in class. Now, go over them a few times, QUICKLY, or do a bit more talking about them with a friend. This procedure will be like singing the same song over and over, and as in the case of the song, you will not forget what you have learned.

6] *Review.*

What! Still more! Well, you would ordinarily review at examination time. We are suggesting that you go over what you have learned and overlearned once a week or every two weeks to keep the information on the tip of your tongue. Reviewing does not take long. Just go over the questions quickly to see if you still know the answers. Recite Portia's speech again. Perhaps you will want to set it to a popular tune or recite it with a beat to relieve the monotony, but do it! Why? Remember, for a minute, trying to recall the name of that fellow who stole all the girls at the dance? You could not recall the name when you wanted to, yet you knew it. Maybe the same thing will happen in class or on a test. It will not happen, however, if you review. The best is yet to come. If you review briefly, but regularly, *your review for any test should not take more than one hour.*

Again, we want to tell you (so you will not be disappointed later) that when you first begin to use these methods you will take *more* time to do your assignments than you did before. But as you learn to use these methods and figure out some short cuts of your own, you will begin to save time. Then your speed of reading will pick up; again, more time saved. You will understand what you have read; no more *re-* and *re-*reading; still more time saved. In other words, you will save time in the long run and still get better grades. Better yet, *you will have learned something.*

Apply what you have learned.

At this point in many study manuals, students are given several projects to complete, the idea being that a demonstration will convince the student that the methods are workable and effective. It has been the author's experience in face-to-face contact with high school students (teaching effective study methods) that there is only one convincing way to prove the effectiveness of these methods: have the student use what is suggested here and compare the results with the results of any other method.

Keeping in mind the explanation of SARTOR, apply the method in studying a prose-type textbook. (Subjects such as mathematics and foreign languages will be discussed later.)

1] *Scan the chapter,* using the summary, the topic headings, and/or your outline book.

2] *Ask yourself questions* about the assignment, and use the questions at the end of the chapter and/or in your outline book. Try to have at least one question for each paragraph. You may prefer to combine scanning and asking by glancing over each paragraph or by skimming the paragraph and making up a question. Write these questions down in your notebook.

3] *Read to answer the questions.* Keep your notebook handy and summarize important points. This is a better system than marking your book (which you are not supposed to do anyhow). After you have finished a short section, summarize it in your own words, and write the summary in your notebook. Now, can you answer the questions you had on that section? How many other questions can you dream up about that topic? Can you answer them?

Hold on for one second. What did you do about that *graph?* Did you look at those *maps* and *tables?* No. Then consider this point: maps, charts, diagrams, and tables are very expensive to print, so publishers want good reasons for putting them in a book. The best reason is that these devices *sum-*

marize important information. Do not look upon a chart as one more page you do not have to read, but look at it as did the old Chinese who said, "One picture is worth a thousand words." Think of how difficult it would be to explain how to assemble a model airplane without a chart or blueprint, or to make a dress without a pattern!

4] *Talk over* with your friends what you have learned, and do not be afraid to recite in class. This is not the army; *do* volunteer every now and then to answer a question, even though no one asked you.

5] *Overlearn and Review*. You may want to combine these two steps. One way of doing this is to organize and systematize all your notes. This does not mean to *copy*. Follow the system given in the chapter on notemaking.

Now that you have gone this far do not lose your original time investment. Go over these notes; *overlearn* them. Go over them again to keep them fresh in your mind. One final point: please do not think that we consider this method to be perfect. The SARTOR method should be used by you as a *guide* to a way of complete study. You will probably find a few little tricks and short cuts of your own. Try out these ideas. If they work, use them; if not, throw them out and look for others. But for your own sake, give this method a good, solid try; then change and improve it so it becomes your servant, but never your master.

CHAPTER 5

Foreign Languages

Why do you think so many people have trouble or, at least, say they have trouble learning foreign languages? Why do you think so many high school students tend to avoid taking foreign languages? It is relatively simple to answer these questions, but before we do, let us give you a brief introduction into the area of studying languages.

The chances are good that if you are reading this section, you have had or anticipate some experience with foreign language(s). The chances are also good that you have had or expect some difficulty with that language. If, at this point, you have had some experience with French, German, Spanish, how much do you know about the most basic fundamentals?

Supply the article with each of the words below (you choose the appropriate language).

French	*German*	*Spanish*
Numérateur	Kur	Continente
Saindoux	Wal	mapa
Objet	Häut	diá
Vérité	Haut	capital
Ebéne	Begriff	cindad

How well did you perform that simple task? Did you know all the articles? Now can you pronounce those words — really pronounce them? Now, let us see what you can do with a few simple sentences.

Translate the following sentences into the foreign language with which you are familiar.

1] I want to give it to you.

2] I am giving it to you.

3] I am hungry.

4] May I have the next dance?

If you have had the difficulties students usually experience with these simple tasks, you may be asking the big question: —

Why study a foreign language?

Since we are going to talk about the study of foreign languages (one of the areas high school students report as being "rough") let us point out that the *subjects* are not difficult — students *make* some subjects, such as languages, difficult. How? Students just do not *learn* the *easy* parts of languages, that is, the elements. Often the elements of a language seem so simple that students do not bother to learn them. But perhaps the student is not entirely to blame. Possibly no one ever *showed* him *how* to learn foreign languages.

Let us look at the student who tells you not to take French (German, Spanish, or Latin) and see why he has had trouble with the foreign language he tried. Possibly he never learned English grammar! It would be difficult for him to write a French subjunctive if he does not know what one looks like in English. But there is also another very basic reason why this student does not learn foreign languages easily. He avoids one of the real essentials for good studying: RECITATION. True, many high school students feel silly and foolish trying to say the French word *pense* without holding their noses or, feel that they will lose a tonsil if they say the German word *hoch* properly. When the instructor tells a student he has to make faces to speak a foreign language, that student is ready to quit. "What about girls?" you may ask; "why do they always do so much better in languages?" We are not so sure they *always* do better, but we are sure it is not because they are naturally better at languages. Maybe girls can speak the languages better (as one wag put it) because they get good practice making faces while putting on their lipstick. "Sure," you say, "so I try, but when I do go through all those motions I sound like a 'bloomin furriner'." Fine; that is the nicest compliment you have paid yourself up to now. You are supposed to sound like a foreigner, remember?

But *why* should you study a foreign language? By the way, reasons such as languages train the mind, help your English vocabulary, make you more intelligent, etc., are at best only secondary reasons. In addition to contributing to your general academic progress and enlarging your vision, the real reasons for taking a foreign language are practical.

One very practical reason for studying foreign languages is that this study will be a very practical check on your native tongue. Each time you attempt to translate from your native tongue into a foreign language you have a very practical test of whether you really understand tenses (past perfect, etc.), moods (e.g., subjunctive), parts of speech and a great variety of rules of grammar. Foreign languages will not only help you to identify your areas of difficulty in your native tongue, but will also help you to improve your command of communication and expression. In addition, those of you who expect to attend college will find out that a foreign language is required or desirable for admission. Those of you who expect to go in for professional training (doctor, dentist, chemist) will find that you will *have* to take a foreign language in your college programs. It might be a good idea to get a head start. Also, many colleges will give you credit for your high school languages if you know them well enough to pass an examination, or in other cases, if you have had enough foreign language preparation. The following excerpt from the University of Maryland, College of Education catalog illustrates this point:

> Required foreign language: 12 semester hours provided the student enters with less than three years of foreign language credit; 6 semester hours, if he enters with three years of such

credit. No foreign language is required of any student who enters with four years of language credit.

In this latter case you would be allowed to take elective courses which are more to your liking. But our job here is not to convince you that you *should* take any course. We should like, however, to convince you that each course offered by your school can be of great advantage to you, and that you *can* pass any course if you learn *how* to study it.

How can I pass my language course?

Instead of answering that question directly, suppose we describe the average student's method of studying his language assignment. Even on the first lesson this student makes the error he will be making all through his course. When he tries to do his first exercise he refers to or keeps looking up the examples and vocabulary, rather than learning them. By the time he gets to Lesson Ten he does not have enough fingers. We think you will know what we mean. This student has one finger in the book at verb endings, one at adjective endings, one at noun endings, one at adverb endings, and a thumb at tenses. There are no fingers left for vocabulary references! There are two big difficulties with learning a language in this way: 1] you spend *more* time looking up and re-looking up references than you would if you had learned the material in the first place, and 2] you will not be allowed to take your book into the tests and examinations with you (at least, not officially). You may have your doubts about reason one above. If you would like to check yourself on this, place a dot (.) before each word each time you look it up in your vocabulary section. After you have done several assignments just take a rough guess at how much time it takes you to look up a word. If you guessed about one half minute, you are correct. Now figure how many times you have looked up a given word and still do not know it. Could you have learned it in that amount of time? Your answer probably is yes. Now consider one additional fact: if you had learned the word in the first place, each additional time you saw it or used it or translated it would be overlearning! This same reasoning applies to grammar and word endings. Learn them right in the beginning, and each use will help in your overlearning. By the end of the school year you will be able to *use* the language if you begin learning this way — to say nothing about the fact that the final examination will be a real snap.

Even though the jokes about the plumber who forgets his tools and has to keep calling the boss for directions were old before Julius Caesar got his first haircut, they get a laugh (if told properly). You see this poor joker going back to the truck for a wrench, then another, etc.; then he has to call the boss for directions. What a dolt, you say. Yet you continue to look up the same old word over and over (return to the truck for tools) and look back at the grammar section to see how a given sentence should be set up (calling the boss for directions). Yes, the words in the vocabulary are your tools, and the rules of grammar are your directions; you cannot do the job well without both. In this case the job is to learn to speak, read, and write the language. Maybe at this point you do not like the job, so you quit! If you are still with us, the suggestions which follow will help you to save time in doing your language assignments, help you to pass exams, and — who would have thought it — you will know something about the language. And you can even have fun working with it.

A good system for learning a foreign language.

Note: If you have come to this point without having read Chapter 3, please go back and read it before you continue. Your understanding of the method given there will be important in understanding the suggestions which follow.

There are two essential differences between studying a language and studying courses such as History, Problems of Democracy, etc. Suppose you had never had a course in History or French. You could open a history book in the middle, read it, understand what is going on, and even pass a test on it.

Try to open a French book in the middle and do one of the exercises. Quite a difference! Yet many students work in just this way. They do not get a good foundation, but they try to build a second floor. The second main difference is that while talking and reciting are important in subjects like history, they are of *primary* importance in languages. If a student does not *participate,* he will not learn very much.

Foreign language text books are set up in a variety of ways, and teachers have different ways of teaching. We shall try to tell you how to apply the SARTOR method to your language studies, regardless of the book and regardless of the teacher's methods. The people connected with FLES (Foreign Languages for Elementary Schools) say that the aim of language teaching should be to teach the student first to speak, then to read, and then to write the language. So you can see how important others consider participating or talking over. (If you are taking Latin you may be wondering how you can go about speaking it. Well, as a secondary-school student the author can recall having quite a bit of fun with a book called MODERN CONVERSATION IN LATIN, and what he learned was a great help in translating CAESAR'S COMMENTARIES.)

1] *Scan.*

Find out what you are supposed to be learning, such as verb endings, how to make adjectives agree with nouns, or what?

2] *Ask.*

Ask how you are going to have to apply what you learn. What are the exercises all about? Look at the other exercises your teacher did not assign.

3] *Read and Talk Over.*

Read the explanation sections carefully. It might help you to know that there are only several *important* things you have to learn about a language:

A] Agreement; that is, how verbs and nouns agree, and how nouns and adjectives agree.

B] Word order; that is, where the adjectives are placed in relation to nouns, where verbs are placed, etc.

C] Vocabulary. In learning both the grammar sections and the vocabulary sections the new material will have to be memorized at first. You should begin your recitation and talking over as soon as you have read. Say the words; repeat the examples given; then say them again. Pay particular attention to these examples because they will use the new words you are supposed to learn, and your vocabulary will mean much more if you can use the words in a sentence.

    1)   Look over your vocabulary. Be sure to learn the article with the noun, and the principal parts of the verb. It is just as easy to learn *das Buch* as to learn *Buch*. But when you learn the article with the noun you automatically know the gender. This rule also applies to French and Spanish. Further, while you are learning your vocabulary be sure that you learn that "the book" means *das Buch* as well as the usual way of learning, i.e., *das Buch* means "the book." Be very careful of correct pronunciation, spelling, accent marks, etc. You know, you could get into trouble with just a slight error. Let us say you are in a South American country and you witness a minor revolution where only several people are made to drop dead. You are called into court as a witness. The Judge asks you, "Who killed these people?" You reply, "*Mato.*" Whereupon they take you out and shoot you. You meant *mató*, but you said *mato*. In your poor Spanish you said "I kill" when you meant "he killed." This would be a rather drastic way to learn *stress*. As far as spelling is concerned, you can also get into trouble. Suppose a Spanish friend of yours writes and asks you what you think of his brother as a business man. You write back that his brother is a *perrito*. The next time the brother

has a big fiesta at his hacienda he pointedly avoids inviting you. Why? Simply because you misspelled a word. You wrote *perrito* (dog) when you meant to write *perito* (expert).

2) Try to learn from five to ten words at a time by saying the word aloud, checking your pronunciation and spelling. Then immediately try to use these words in a sentence or phrase.

3) Take another five or ten words and learn them in the way that was just explained. Now, go over both lists. When you have learned the whole vocabulary, turn immediately to the English-to-foreign-language assignment and do it. Concentrate on this aspect because once you master English-to-foreign-language the reverse will be easy. While you are doing your assignment *write down* on a card (or in your notebook) any word you missed. Write the English on one side of the card and the foreign word on the other side. Now go over these words until you know them. One precaution: although we suggest you learn your vocabulary by using the words, some of you may still learn them by reciting a long list. If you insist upon doing this, put the words on cards. Each time you go over the list shuffle the cards so you do *not* learn the words in just one order. Learning words in a list can lead only to a memorized list; the individual words will not be meaningful to you.

4) *Talk over.* If you have been studying your assignment properly you have been doing a lot of talking. But there is more to do. Make a definite effort to repeat what your teacher says in class. Try to *anticipate* what he/she is going to say. Answer all questions. If you are not asked the question, answer it under your breath. If your school uses some electrical gadget such as a phonograph, tape recorder, or one of the other devices available, pay particular attention to pronunciation and expressions, and listen to the *way* things are said.

Most of all, try to use the language in your everyday

conversations. Try using the language on your classmates to ask them to go for a ride, to sit down, or to pass the catsup or salt (when you are having your meals in the school cafeteria). Try to translate common, everyday expressions into the language you are studying. Call your friends names (genteel ones, of course) if you must, but whatever you do, *practice* and *use* the language.

5) *Overlearn.* Once a week go back to your old assignments and take one sentence from each (take a different one each time you go back); see if you can still do what is asked.

6) *Review.* If you have studied properly, you will find that when you review you can do the exercises and translations much more quickly than you did in the beginning, to say nothing of more correctly. We believe language study will begin to be like athletics. In the beginning you will not enjoy the exercises, but you will enjoy playing in the game — in this case actually being able to use the language. Give yourself a chance to find out that learning, too, can be fun. Give it a try!

CHAPTER **6**

History
and Other Social Sciences

How practical is learning history?

Jim Olmea and his wife visited a noted sculptor who was in the process of completing a huge clay model of a battle memorial prior to its being cut into stone. Jim, an amateur historian and arms buff, pointed out to the sculptor that the muskets shown in the clay model were not in use during the period supposedly depicted by the huge piece of statuary. The correction saved the noted sculptor a great amount of criticism, embarrassment and even possible rejection of his work.

The practical applications you will be able to make of the historical information you learn may not be quite so dramatic as the example given above, but they may be more enlightening and satisfying for you. You will find that you will have a better background for interpreting current civic problems. Although you may not think so at the moment, you will develop a certain amount of pride in being an unusually well-informed citizen. And you will be able to have a certain amount of fun checking on and correcting errors made in motion picture and television productions.

As was said, you may not believe the statements just made, especially the one about having fun with history. The statements, however, are true. The author has been able to prove the point to his own satisfaction by applying the techniques

87

which will follow and proving the point with such unlikely groups as rough and ready infantry soldiers, young children and completely uninterested high school students.

Of course not every student who reads or who applies the methods suggested in this book will become an avid student of history, but most will find out that they can *learn* the subject relatively painlessly and apply what they learn. And, as in the case with most other subjects, once a student begins actually to learn a subject he begins to enjoy it.

How is it possible to assure such interest in history?

History is really a true story of a given period of time, of a country, or a person or event. Of course, history is really more than *just* a story. Some events of history are thrilling adventures, some events are romantic while others are dull. The category a given event falls into depends on the person reading about the event. To the proper young lady the events of the "old west" may be barbaric, to the red-blooded young male they may be better than the best motion-picture production.

It is sometimes difficult to understand how any person can read about Caesar's legions drawn up for battle without feeling a certain thrill . . . or of visualizing the raggle-taggle, suffering Continental Army overcoming the misery and suffering at Valley Forge to defeat Cornwallis and his army at Yorktown without getting a feeling of national pride. These things are especially difficult to understand when we consider the millions of persons who flock to see Hollywood productions based on the same periods of history. The Hollywood producers recognize the appeal of great events of history and have poured the greatest sums ever into pictures about these events.

As an individual you have as much imagination as the next person. *All* of the events so expensively produced by Hollywood are available to you in the history books in your school and local library. All you have to do is to read and let your imagination run wild and you can "see" some of the greatest productions the world has ever or will ever know.

But what about studying history in school?

Why should the events shown in various productions suddenly become uninteresting or dull when presented in school? The answer is they do not! The difference is that in the *study* of history you are expected to know the facts, not merely be entertained by them. Your teacher is trying to get you to learn enough information to give you the background to become a well-informed, well-educated citizen.

The gripe that many students seem to have is that they are held responsible for too many small items: names, dates, places, etc., etc., etc. But these items are the tools of history; these are the items that have been so painstakingly researched to make the Hollywood production so spectacular and so "interesting." But, even so, the student with such a gripe is concentrating on the minutiae and not what the names, dates, etc., contribute. They never learn how to *associate* the minutiae into a story.

Possibly you are one of the students who could not care less about dates. But let us look at what a difference a date can make. Suppose we learn that a certain gentleman designed a submarine and an airplane. So what! It is done every day. But suppose we learn that the gentleman was Leonardo Da Vinci and that he designed these machines in the early 1500's. Or suppose we find that another person measured the diameter of the Earth, and did so fairly accurately. Suppose further we learn that the person was Eratosthenes and that he did his measuring between the years 276-194 B.C. Could you do as well right now?

But how can anyone learn these things without becoming bogged down in too many details?

The problem in studying history like the problem in studying any other subject is that many students expect to read or be exposed to a subject and to *absorb*. History like any other subject must be studied. The SARTOR method is especially well-suited for the study of history and the other social sciences. There are, however, one or two special techniques to help you to learn the basic facts and to associate them in such a way that they will become and remain meaningful.

First, you should get a general idea of the period about which you are going to read. This can be done by using an "outline book" prior to reading the text. Here you will be able to identify and have some questions about the important persons, places, and dates. If you are going to make notes, list the names, etc. on the left side of a sheet of paper (see below) and to the right of the name make a brief list or outline of what you have learned from your outline book. Now, when you read your text book, according to the suggestions in Chapter 3, make additional notes on what you have read. As has been suggested before, be sure these notes are *in your own words*.

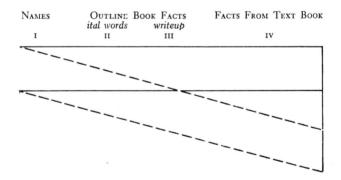

NAMES	OUTLINE BOOK FACTS *ital words*	*writeup*	FACTS FROM TEXT BOOK
I	II	III	IV

Notice as you make notes on your text-book reading, the facts about the first name overlap the facts about the second name. This technique sets up associations in all directions. Let us take a hypothetical case and see how this technique actually works.

Suppose you are about to read about the Federalist period of United States history, you might begin by reading a very brief statement of the period in an outline book. The following write-up illustrates such a brief statement:

PERIOD OF THE FEDERALISTS 1789-1800

Era of conservation.

The adoption of the Constitution of 1787, essentially a conservative document, ushered in an era of conservation. The government in this period was dominated by the Federalist party whose leader and chief spokesman was *Alexander Hamilton*. Hamilton spoke for a rule by the aristocracy, believing the common man too ignorant to be capable of wise, self-rule. Hamilton believed that for the most part a government controlled and administered by the "wiser" aristocrats and/or landed gentry would be of greater benefit to all concerned. In spite of his brilliance, wisdom and devotion to duty, Hamilton allowed his aristocratic leanings to carry him too far. The general populace as well as many individuals of influence believed that Hamilton had monarchial leanings and finally displaced him and his ideas at the polls with the acceptance of and election of the liberal Thomas Jefferson.

Notice in reading the brief statement that the Constitution is mentioned; the names Federalist, Alexander Hamilton and Thomas Jefferson are also mentioned. As you read further you will hear such names as Washington, John Adams, Henry Knox, to name a few. You will also hear about some activities of Congress and Hamilton's and Jefferson's philosophies. You will also see why the names Hamilton and Jefferson are the two names that appear in the very brief write-up.

Now let us look at an actual application of the overlapping triangle principle. We shall continue with the Federalist period. Please remember that what is to follow is only a brief presentation, space does not permit the writing of a full chapter of history, only a method of studying such a chapter. Please go through the following procedure *very* carefully reading first column I then II, III and finally IV.

If you refer to the illustration following, you will notice you have identified all of the important persons, events, etc. in Column I. In Column II and III you have most of the information you will need for factual objective questions. In

I	II
1789 Inauguration of Washington	Unanimously elected President John Adams, Vice-President
Establishment of Government	Congress suggested many titles and procedures . . . origin of many ceremonial procedures. Origin of cabinet, three executive departments, court system, and revenue measures. Adoption of Bill of Rights.
Thomas Jefferson (1743-1826)	Dreamer Government by the common man. Rights of the individual and States. Theorist and writer.
Alexander Hamilton (1757-1804)	Practical man of action. Government by aristocracy. Sound fiscal procedures. Strong central government. Realist

III

Washington was a strong leader who was trusted by and commanded respect from most of the responsible men in the government. He was a rather formal and austere man who was neither a top administrator nor facile politician. He could and did, however, work with the Congress.

In this period the Congress began establishing government procedures and precedents. At first, the new government attempted to have the Chief Executive addressed by such titles as "Excellency" and "Elective Majesty," and, while the resolution suggesting these titles failed to pass, many of the Senate's ceremonial procedures originated during this period. Congress also "originated the Cabinet" by the establishment of three executive departments: State, War, and Treasury. It also established the Office of the Attorney General, the Supreme Court, and District Courts. It was also during this time that the Bill of Rights was adopted.

One man prominent in the government was Thomas Jefferson, a brilliant political theorist. Although master of many academic pursuits, he was a poor administrator, having left the State of Virginia (of which he had been Governor) in somewhat less than ship-shape order. Jefferson was in favor of government by the masses and individual rights. He was a charming and cultured gentleman who was interested more in contentment than efficiency.

Alexander Hamilton, a brilliant and practical man was in favor of a strong central government controlled by the landed gentry and aristocracy, whom he felt to be the only persons wise enough to pilot the "Ship of State." Hamilton was at his best setting up plans and procedures and watching them work. He was a financial wizard who was in favor of high finance, big business, and big trading organizations. In spite of his brilliance and personal charm, his hot temper led to his political downfall and to his untimely death.

IV

In this period Washington was looked to for guidance as he had been during the dark years of the revolution. His aloofness from parties and factions made him trusted by the various factions in the government. As was "the general," the President was formal and dignified, lending both formality and dignity to the new government. His devotion to duty was witnessed by his long hours of work and rewarded by the trust of all fair and responsible men.

When the Congress began to put together the skeleton of the new government, it was decided that the persons who were to head the new agencies were to be appointed by the President and confirmed by the Senate. By now, however, political parties had begun to appear. Different men and different factions had different ideas as to how the government should be constructed. It was not unusual then, that men of different political ideas should appear in the government.

When the Congress created the first departments, the men available to fill these posts were of different opinions. When the Department of State was created, Washington appointed Thomas Jefferson to fill this important post.

Jefferson, a man of little organizational ability, was, however, a man of thought and philosophy and the Dean of political thinkers and writers in his own time. An individualist to the last, Jefferson was in favor of the rights of the individual and of States' Rights. He did not favor a strong central government, nor did he favor anything "BIG," be they government, manufacturers, banks, or trading organizations.

Jefferson was in direct opposition to Alexander Hamilton, the man Washington appointed to head the newly-formed Department of the Treasury. Hamilton, in contrast with the slow-moving Jefferson, was an energetic man of action. Both men were brilliant but with such opposing views that it is no wonder that not only the men but their views were the bases for long-lived conflicts. Hamilton, a genius at organizing and executing, was a Federalist and in favor of a strong central government. He was also a financial genius and the greatest Treasury head in American History. Not only was he able to devise a plan to pay off the national debt but also to assume and to pay off the debts left by the individual states. While brilliant, engaging, handsome, and socially adept, Hamilton was also quick-tempered and petulant when crossed. He was quick to take the offensive and this facet of his personality led to his early and untimely death in a duel with Aaron Burr.

Column IV you have the base for "thought," objective questions and for essay and/or discussion questions. The student who wishes to expand the triangles has only to add Column V and makes notes from additional texts and/or reference books.

Again, if you refer to the illustration following you will notice that the "associations" go in all directions from names to events and vice-versa. In addition, it is difficult to think of one name or event without thinking of most of the other names and events. Try it! Take any one of the names or events and you will find it *difficult not* to think of the other names and events. Quite a difference, is it not! Quite a difference having difficulty *not* recalling events rather than having difficulty recalling the events. This little demonstration should prove the method to you. It should be pointed out, however, that it is not necessary to go into an elaborate scheme, drawing triangles etc. You may want to follow the graphic procedure but on the other hand you may wish to modify this procedure so that it fits more easily on a page.

You should also constantly try to use what you already know to help formulate questions and to assimilate what you are reading. In the current case, a good example of using what is known to formulate questions is found in applying your knowledge of the fact that elections for President of the United States takes place every four years. Now, for example, how do you explain the fact that Washington was inaugurated in 1798 and Jefferson was elected in 1800? Many other such incidents will be found if you are constantly aware of and apply what you already know. You should also be aware that the more you apply this procedure, the more you *will* know and be able to apply.

Try to ask questions about points as they come up — e.g., how, when, where, why, etc. Try to keep looking for the tie-in between what you are reading and what you have read. Try to make as many associations as you can, that is, tie in the facts you are learning with as many other facts and descriptions as possible. In that way mere mention of any fact or thought will, as you have already seen, bring to mind many other persons, events, etc. with no effort on your part.

At first this method will be time-consuming, but if you followed the steps carefully you will really know something about the Federalist period. If, in addition, you were to read an actual text chapter on this period, you would have not only the facts but the flavor of the period. But, as was said this seems like a time-consuming process; actually it is not. Once you become familiar with the procedure and apply it, almost automatically you will learn and remember history once you study it.

Notice also that if you follow the additional suggestions you will be able to answer questions such as:

> *How* did Hamilton solve the debt problem? Who was Aaron Burr, why did he provoke a duel with Hamilton, and what finally happened to Burr? Hamilton believed in rule by the aristocracy; how was this idea used in the right to vote controversy prevalent in the 1960's?

You will also have some background on why Hamilton wanted to establish and did establish the Bank of the United States and why Jefferson opposed such a bank. And if you are one of the more interested students you will find background and possibly a lead into much deeper questions concerning the long, practical and philosophical arguments and questions about Federalism vs Jeffersonian Democracy, Republic vs Democracy and some bases for current fiscal policies.

NOTE: Did you explain the question about how Washington was inaugurated in 1798 and Jefferson was elected in 1800? Did you think that this "might" be a typographical error or a printer's error? In this case it *was* an error, an intentional "error."

Other social sciences such as American Government, Problems of Democracy, Sociology, and Economics can be handled by application of the system just presented. Space does not permit a separate chapter on each of these subjects, nor is there any real reason for such a presentation. You now have the system, all you have to do is apply it.

CHAPTER 7

Mathematics

Suppose you were asked to solve this problem:

A man invested $30,000 for one year at simple interest; one portion was invested at 5% and the remainder at 2%. How much did he invest at each rate if the total return was at the rate of 4%? [1]

Can you solve this relatively simple problem? If not, do you know why you cannot solve it?

What are the two main steps involved in solving any problem?

Some time ago the author witnessed the following scene between a mother and her very young son. The boy was searching through the drawers of a cabinet when his mother asked him, "What are you looking for?" The boy answered, "I'll know when I find it." This example may sound like a far cry from studying and learning mathematics, but actually it is very similar to an experience the author had while attempting to help a "special-study-problem" student with his Solid Geometry. This student had been "given up" by two mathematics tutors because in their opinion he "just couldn't get Solid." After a great amount of work, the author was also ready to give up because there seemed to be *something* which kept the student from learning Geometry; there was definitely a special problem. This student could not solve very simple

[1] Newsom & Eves, (17), pp. 266, 267.

problems involving perimeters, areas, etc. Finally, in desperation, the author asked the student several questions: "What is a perimeter? What is an area?" It did not seem possible that not knowing these definitions could be a *college* student's problem, but it was!

The first step in helping this student to learn geometry was to have him look up the definitions of these basic words. He was then to attempt to work out his mathematics problems and return for further tutoring. No further tutoring was necessary. When the student found out *what* he was looking for he was able to work the problems. To make a long story short, he passed the course and learned the first step in solving any problem. *What* am I looking for?

A second problem which confronts many students is *how* to solve mathematics problems. They do not know how to begin to work the problems because *they do not know which operations to perform*. Possibly, one explanation for this fact is that the average student never learns to *understand* what he does (or which operations he performs) in solving simple problems. Suppose we take a very simple example. A boy goes to the store and buys a 59¢ model airplane, and pays the clerk with a dollar. What mathematical process (operation) does the boy use to find out how much change he should get? He subtracts. We all know how to do this problem, but are we really aware that we *subtract*? This question was asked of a number of high school graduates, and many of them fumbled for quite a while before they came up with the correct answer. Many of them gave the correct amount of change the boy should receive, but they failed to answer the question.

But what what has all of this to do with learning algebra or business math?

In a nutshell, "it" is the crux of learning mathematics; you must know *what* to look for and *how* to work a problem before you can solve it. Anyone who learns the basic fundamentals of how to work problems can be at least mildly successful at doing mathematics. You do not have to be or have some special kind of genius to master arithmetic or algebra; *you do*, however, *have to work.* But if you follow the suggestions made in this chapter, your work will become much easier. In addition, you will get better grades, and even more important, learn how to *master* mathematics. Please keep in mind that this chapter is meant to help you to gain confidence and to teach you how to study mathematics. Keep these facts in mind, and your teacher will have at least an even chance to teach you how to do mathematics.

Why the special concern about mathematics?

The author has found that mathematics is another of those subjects which is considered to be difficult. Consequently, students avoid mathematics, only to find that when they get out into the business world or go to college much of their basic education has been neglected. Sure, they took a course or so, but it was too hard; so they dropped it. Now they are sorry. These students *knew* they "couldn't do math"; consequently, they had failed before they started. However, the author has also found that many of these students who "never could do math" actually get good grades in their mathematics courses once they are given the confidence to try and are shown how to work. So, in one respect some students are correct; they cannot do mathematics, now. But they are incorrect in assuming that they cannot do mathematcics, PERIOD. The author has proved to his own satisfaction and to the satisfaction of a great many students that *just about anyone who really tries can learn to do mathematics.*

Suppose for a minute you are now of the opinion that you want to learn algebra (geometry, business math). How do you go about learning what to do and how to do it? Most students complain about the word problems. But after all, word problems are the crux of mathematics. Anyone with any *basic* algebra training and who knows arithmetic should be able to solve this problem:

$$0.05x + 600 - 0.02x = 1200$$

But can this same person set up this equation when given the problem mentioned at the beginning of this section?

Let us consider a more simple example of the same kind of thing for now. A student in the fifth grade is asked to solve the following problem:

> Mr. Peterson purchased 30,000 acres of land for $1,200,-000. How much did he pay for one acre?

The grade-school student is usually completely upset by what is an acre, what is $1,200,000, etc. The big numbers "throw him" before he has a chance to look at the problem. He does not know what process (operation) to use or what he is trying to find out. If we ask the same student a similar problem we can get him to think. Take this problem:

> You just bought 5 candy bars for 25¢. How much did each bar cost?

He answers, "five cents." We ask, "How did you find that?" He says, "I just know." Finally, after several tries, he gets the idea and says, "Oh, I divided." When we repeat the two problems together he begins to see the similarity. He sees that the problem about Mr. Peterson's acres *sounds* like the candy-bar problem. Now he knows how to do the problem, but we did not show him how. In the beginning the boy allowed himself to be fluffed by things which did not really affect the problem. The problem to which we referred might have involved lexicons (instead of acres) selling for kopecs (instead of dollars) and the child still could have solved the problem if he had known *where* and *how* to look. In fact, you would find that once this fifth-grader learns what to do and how to do it he can solve some rather unusual arithmetic problems.

Algebra problems are very similar to the simple arithmetic examples we just used. Students seem to have difficulty in *translating* from English to algebra. This means they have trouble building the formula from a simple statement of a problem. These students do not know "what they are looking for." Further, they do not know how to do the work after they learn what to do. Why should this be? Well, one good answer is that students seldom spend enough time on fundamentals and on *studying* the examples given in the textbook. Sure, they give a quick look at the book, and then go on to the homework assignment. This statement is easy to prove. The next time you have a mathematics assignment do your studying; then for the first problem try to work the example (demonstration problem) *without looking at your book.*

What are the secrets of learning any skill?

If you wanted to learn to be a good swimmer you would practice the fundamentals until you could do them without thinking. And, you would practice these skills *every time* you went swimming. In mathematics the fundamentals *seem* so easy that only a few people take them seriously. These few people learn mathematics while the others never learn how to do even the most basic operations. Think of learning how to do mathematics in the same way as building a house. The fundamentals are the foundation. If you have either no foundation or a weak one, your building will fall down at some point. Another thing to keep in mind is that the higher the building is to be (the higher you wish to go in mathematics) the stronger the foundation *must* be.

So far we have emphasized one point: *you must learn fundamentals.* But there is another important point: *You must decide that you are going to work* if you want to learn or have to learn mathematics. You will have to give up the idea that some people can do mathematics and others cannot. As was said before, anyone can be at least moderately successful if he tries. So first, if you decide to work, you can succeed; if you decide you will *not* work, you have already failed. Second, you are going to learn the fundamentals of mathematics; you are going to learn addition, subtraction, and the meanings of all words you do not already know. Third, you are going to *study* the illustrations in each chapter *before* you try to work any of the problems. Fourth, you will try to *apply* what you have just learned and are about to learn to the problems in your mathematics homework assignments.

What should I do?

If you are a student who is already having trouble with mathematics your first job is to pin-point the trouble or troubles. This can be done in one or two ways: *a*] you can look over your old homework sheets and quizzes to find out what mistakes you do make, and/or *b*] you can have your school counselor give you a *diagnostic* mathematics test to discover your troubles. In either case, it would be wise to check with your mathematics teacher to get his suggestions. The next step, naturally, would be to work on the consistent errors. (Later in this section we shall tell you how to eliminate many of these errors.) On the other hand, if you are a student who is just starting a new mathematics course, just follow the directions we are going to give.

Whether or not you will be able to do mathematics will depend on how well you master the fundamentals. Usually, students know how to do addition, subtraction, and other operations of this kind, but very few students are careful enough in these operations. They usually make careless or "dumb" mistakes. So, your first step will be to learn to add, subtract, multiply, and divide *quickly* and *correctly*. Second, you will have to learn *exactly* what is meant by new terms such as *factoring, progressions, rate, etc.*, and in geometry, terms such as *area, perimeter, volume, congruent,* etc. A student who does not understand the terminology of the subject he is studying will not understand the explanations, nor will he know what is being asked in the problems.

Now you are really ready to begin studying. How can you apply what you have learned up to this point to the study of mathematics? Well, how many times have you understood (or thought you understood) the explanation of some problems given in class by your teacher, only to find that when you started your homework that night you just could not do it? You ask yourself, "Did I really know what he (the teacher) was talking about?" The answer is probably yes, you did. But by waiting too long to apply what you learned, you *forgot*. However, this is what you would have predicted from what you know about learning and forgetting. So, your first step will be to get at your homework *as soon as possible* after your mathematics class. Ordinarily, if you can begin your homework *immediately* after class you will save more than enough time to carry out the steps we are about to suggest.

Now, how do you go about applying SARTOR to the study of mathematics? Fortunately, most mathematics books are set up so that if you follow directions you *almost* automatically accomplish what you accomplish when you use SARTOR.

♦ HERE ARE A FEW SUGGESTIONS which will help you in your assignments.

1] *Scan* the lesson to get a general idea of what the author is going to explain. Maybe it would be better at times if you studied only part of the assignment, or perhaps it is a short assignment which you can do in one sitting. In any case, plan your work.

2] *Ask* yourself what you are going to be doing in this assignment. (Keep *what* and *how* in mind as you carry out this step.) Look over the exercises and illustrative problems, *paying particular attention to the problems assigned to you as homework*. In this way you will get some idea about what you will be looking for in these types of problems.

3] *Read* the explanations, *paying particular attention* not only to the meanings of new words and the explanations, but also to the illustrative problem or problems. You are now at the critical point in learning mathematics. The next step is the important one, and yet it is usually omitted by students. LEARN THE ILLUSTRATIVE PROBLEM! As you study the illustrative problem, keep in mind the problems you have looked over in the "Ask" phase of your studying. How does the illustrative problem apply to the problems in the exercises? How can it help you to solve these problems? Keep looking for similarities between the illustrative problem and the problems in the exercises. At first this step will be rather time-consuming, but as you learn the trick of applying what you learn in the explanations to what you have to do, later you will find that the time consumed in doing your homework will be cut down appreciably.

4] *Test* yourself (instead of talking over). You test yourself by closing your book and seeing if you can *completely* reproduce the illustrative problem without looking at your book. You should also check yourself to see if you know and understand the meanings of the new words, functions, operations, etc. mentioned in your lesson. If, at this point, you can pass your own test, you are ready for the next step. If you do not pass this test, *go back and study some more.*

5] *Overlearn* by applying what you have just learned. Work the assigned problems. As soon as you are sure you know how to work them, begin to prepare for your next quiz or examination by working the remainder of your assignment *against time.* This suggestion is made because many students seem to be able to do mathematics problems when they have *plenty of time,* but when faced with the same problems on an examination they have difficulty. These students are either unable to finish all the problems on the examination, or they hurry and make careless or "dumb" mistakes. The system of practicing homework against time has been tried with many students who have had trouble finishing examinations; it has been found to be amazingly simple and effective. And it has also been found to be the simplest and most effective way of overcoming the "dumb" mistakes made while hurrying. The best way to apply this system is to predict how many problems (of the kind you are working) your teacher would include on an hour examination. Assume your homework problems are a test, and work them in the same amount of time you would have for a test. Now, correct the problems to see if and where you made mistakes and/or where you had difficulty. Again practice the steps which gave you trouble.

6] *Review.* The most efficient way to review your mathematics is to work (at the end of each week) *at least* one of each type of problem you have had during the week, *against time*. But, work a problem you have not tried before. Then at the end of the month repeat this process; that is, work *at least* one of each type of problem you have had during the past month. This system of reviewing is suggested because it will help you to keep all types of problems at your finger tips at all times. You will be ready for "pop" quizzes, and it will be unnecessary for you to conduct any big reviews before examinations.

"Fine," you say, "but I still have trouble. I can do everything but the word problems." You are not alone. Quite a few students have this complaint, and when they do they are usually referring to algebra problems. So, let us use the same problems stated on page 75 and see how we *should* go about solving it.

> A man invested $30,000 for one year at simple interest; one portion was invested at 5% and the remainder at 2%. How much did he invest at each rate if the total return was at the rate of 4%? [1]

The first problem *as seen by the student* is: which formula do I use, or how do I translate this problem into a formula? The question is fine, but the student is ahead of himself. He should first ask himself, what does the problem ask? What do I have to find? Do I know of a similar problem which I have already solved? What is the unknown? Then, how can I put down in algebraic terms what I find out from the word problem?

If you tried to work this problem you would decide that an equation is necessary to solve it. So, let us follow Newsom and Eves' suggested solution.[1]

> In attempting to answer the question of this problem through the use of an equation, it is first essential to discover what quantities must be equal. After some consideration, it is evident that the skeleton of the desired equation is (interest

1 Newsom, C. V. and Eves, H., AN INTRODUCTION TO COLLEGE MATHEMATICS, 1954. Prentice-Hall, Inc., Englewood Cliffs, New Jersey. Reprinted by permission.

from the portion invested at 5%) + (interest from the portion invested at 2%) = (interest if the whole sum had been invested at 4%).

This, however, is not an algebraic equation. How do you go about translating this statement into *algebra*?

Since the portion invested at 5% is unknown, it will be designated by x; it follows, then, that the interest from this particular portion is 0.05x.

Since the remainder of the money is invested at 2%, (30,000 − x) must be the remainder and (0.02) (30,000 − x) is the interest received from the part invested at 2%. The interest obtained if the whole sum had been invested at 4% is obviously (0.04) (30,000) or 1200.

It is now possible to symbolize completely the equation in the form

$$0.05x + 0.02\,(30{,}000 - x) = 1200.$$

Which may be rewritten as

$$0.05x + 600 - 0.02x = 1200$$

or

$$0.03x + 600 = 1200$$

By the fundamental theorem, this equation is known to possess a root. Thus the statement

$$0.03x + 600 = 1200$$

is a true equality if x denotes that root. Therefore, $0.03x = 600$ (subtracting 600 from each member) $3x = 60{,}000$ multiplying each number by 100); and $x = 20{,}000$ (dividing each member by 3).

It follows, as a consequence, that the desired value of the root is 20,000, which means that the amount of money invested at 5% is $20,000. Of course, the amount of money invested at 2% must be $10,000. These results completely satisfy the conditions of the original problem.

It is recommended to the student of mathematics that he should always set up his work in about as detailed fashion as that given above. This facilitates careful thought and the thorough analysis that is essential.

This example is included to show you that even the mathematician recommends not only a careful analysis of the problem, but a careful step-by-step solution. You will find that once you understand the process of learning what to look for and how to look, your difficulties in solving mathematics problems will be greatly diminished.

HOW CAN I SET UP A GOOD PROCEDURE?

Immediately following this section you will find a step-by-step set of directions on HOW TO LEARN TO SOLVE PROBLEMS. The section just mentioned is not meant to be a set of cook-book directions but rather a method for learning how to solve problems. Use these directions in your study of mathematics. For the high school student who wishes to study mathematics seriously, i.e., major in mathematics, physical science or engineering, the author suggests that he obtain a copy of HOW TO SOLVE IT (11) and Newsom and Eves (9) and study the suggestions given in these very valuable books.

One final suggestions for beating the "matematics jitters" is taken up in Chapter 9, "Tests and Examinations." When you have read and applied the methods given in the present chapter, and when you have learned how to take examinations, you should be in a position to learn *enough* mathematics and perform well enough to suit *your* purpose.

HOW TO LEARN TO SOLVE PROBLEMS

STEP 1 *Study* the problem. What does it ask?

What are you asked to do? What information is given to help you to do what you are asked to do?

First, study your text and consider what your instructor has said in class. What are you trying to learn to do? Now, get the general idea of how such problems are stated and set up by *learning* the demonstration problem and/or the problem(s) explained in class. After you understand the demonstration problem(s), close your book and work the demonstration problem (see pages 83-84 of this chapter) to be sure you understand *all* steps and *all new* terminology.

STEP 2 Connect the problems you have been assigned to solve with a problem you already know.

You should always try to connect what you are learning with what you already know. In other words, always try to make your material meaningful.

Examine *all* of the problems at the end of the chapter you are studying. Regardless of which problems you are assigned, select the problem which looks *most* like the demonstration problem(s) given in the text and/or in class. Discover the similarities between the problem you have selected and the demonstration problem; see how it can be "translated" into algebra (or geometry) according to the directions you have just learned; when possible, draw a figure according to the directions given in the problem. When you have solved this problem you will have two MODELS. Continue the process just suggested until you are sure you understand how to solve these kinds of problems. Now, complete your homework.

As you set up each problem, explain to yourself *why* you are performing each operation. As you work the problem explain each step you are performing. In other words, be sure you *understand* what you are doing and why you are doing it and *not* merely working by rote.

STEP 3 Work against time.

After you are sure you *understand* and *know* how to work the problems decide how many of this type of problem you would be expected to solve in a one-hour test. Work several problems against time to be sure you can work both quickly and carefully.

As in all other learning situations you should practice the material or skill the way you are going to be using it. Practicing your mathematics against time will help you to avoid what students call "dumb" or "stupid" mistakes. These "dumb" or "stupid" mistakes are usually made when a student is trying to work much faster than the rate to which he has become accustomed or at which he has been working.

STEP 4   Check your work.

Be sure your answer is correct. In the event, after you have given a particular problem a real good try, you cannot solve it or get the correct solution, put that problem aside. Try working another problem. Now go back to the one with which you have been having difficulty. If you get into a real "rut," that is, cannot seem to accomplish anything, put aside your mathematics for a while, study another subject and return to mathematics later.

STEP 5   Generalize your solution.

Look over all of the problems you have worked. Try to understand the *general* way in which such problems are stated. Now, *you* try to make up a few problems of your own. Once you have reached this point you will have a good understanding of the particular topic of mathematics you are studying.

ADDENDUM

If you experience difficulty in understanding the principles of algebra, the author suggests that you purchase a copy of ADVENTURES IN ALGEBRA (9). This self-help text will help you to teach yourself the underlying concepts and ideas of algebra and will give you a basic introduction to the use of symbols and numbers. If you are at the point where you need to *learn* algebra or to get a good review of algebra, the author suggests that you obtain a copy of TEMAC, FIRST YEAR ALGEBRA (15). TEMAC consists of programmed learning materials which will enable you to teach yourself if you are willing to follow directions and to spend the time necessary to do the work.

CHAPTER 8

Studying Sciences

How can anyone remember so many facts?

Jane Sowanski, in a fit of frustration over a failure in her zoology test, asked:

> How can I memorize so many facts? They ask for so many details! How can I remember how to trace a drop of blood from the left toe to the right ear – or from the right index finger to the nose – or – what's the use! They can ask thousands and thousands of tracings; I can't memorize them all. And that's only part of it; there are all those bones and cells, and – what's the use! I just can't get it.

Yet, within one month of making statements like the one above, Jane was getting better than 90's on her Zoology tests and made a 95 on the final.

Granted, Jane was more frustrated and disgusted than most students. Yet she was rather typical of many students who experience difficulty in studying science. And, her improvement, while better than most students' improvement, was typical of what students are able to do when they follow the methods of studying science given below.

But first, let us consider the fact that one way of defining science is that science is classified and/or systematized information. Yet, classifying or organizing information seems to be one of the last things a student will do when he is studying science. The average student who experiences difficulty in studying the Biological Sciences usually does so because he is trying to memorize too many unrelated facts. Actually, he often memorizes the same fact in several different ways without seeing or realizing the connection.

Even though the facts of science are meaningfully related, many students seem to do their best to memorize facts in isolation. They make little or no effort to relate what they are learning to what they have learned. They make no effort to use what they are learning, i.e., apply it to their own environment or to their own bodies.

How can you learn the facts of science so that you can organize, use, and apply them?

In order to learn science so that it will be both easy to learn and meaningful, these important steps are necessary:

1] *Step one* is to find the central or main idea of the area being studied.

2] *Step two* is to use what you already know and have recently learned as a basis for what you are learning. This step is fundamental in *getting an education* as well as mere course passing.

3] *Step three* is to apply what you learn to your own environment and where possible, to your own body. Make what you are learning meaningful and useful to you in your understanding of the workings of your environment, or the inhabitants of that environment, and of your own body.

Let us go back to a specific problem, the one mentioned in the opening paragraph, of this chapter, and see how we can apply the three steps of learning science to tracing a drop of blood — from *anyplace* to *anyplace*. To get at *Step one*, the central or main idea of the section, the author usually asks the question: "In the higher animals, for a drop of blood to go *from* anyplace to anyplace, what *must* that drop of blood do — and/or where must it go in order to be 'circulated'?" The answer is, the blood must be *pumped* by the *heart*. In the process of being *pumped*, the blood is *aerated* or *purified* by being *pumped* through the *lungs*. Consequently, a student should first learn how a drop of blood goes through the *heart* and *lung* cycle. Regardless of where the blood is *coming from* or *going to* it will always *make this trip* in a complete cycle.

If you were learning this particular cycle you might visualize the blood going through the following *pumping* and *purifying* stages.

FIG. 3   *Diagrammatic representation of heart and lungs circulation.*

This might be done to see how the heart works. Later you could visualize the process like this:

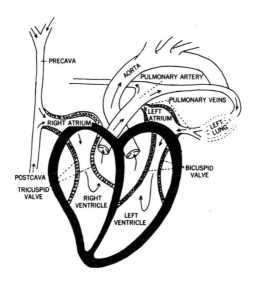

FIG. 4   *Simplified diagram of heart and lungs circulation.*

Notice, if you count the parts you have learned in this little demonstration you have eleven parts. Ordinarily, you will not have to use more than twenty or twenty-two parts (organs and/or vessels) to trace a drop of blood *from* anyplace to anyplace. Therefore, just knowing the heart-lung cycle will give you approximately 50% of any blood tracing.

If you had been studying a chapter on circulation of the blood, you would also have noticed one other central idea: *Arteries* always carry blood away from the heart and *veins* always carry blood to or toward the heart. These facts would put us in a position to use what we already know and, with the learning of several additional parts, be able to trace a drop of blood *from* any main area of the body *to* any main area of the body.

Let us now look at the diagram of the skeleton (Figure 5) because, since the study of the skeleton usually procedes the study of the organs, muscles, etc., it is assumed that you would have learned the bones of the body. Now, look at Figure 6. How many blood vessels have the same names, e.g., Femur — Femoral Vein, Femoral Artery?

TIBIA	Anterior tibial vein
	Anterior tibial artery
	Posterior tibial vein
	Posterior tibial artery
FEMUR	Femoral vein
	Femoral artery
ILIUM	Iliac vein and artery
CLAVICLE	Subclavian vein and artery
RADIUS	Radial vein and artery
ULNA	Ulnar vein and artery

Of course, not all the similarities have been noted, just enough to give you the idea of how to add what you are learning to what you already know. If you now learn *Cava* (pre and post), *Jugular* (internal and external), *Carotid* (internal and external), *Brachial* and the *Aorta*, you can trace a drop of blood from one end of the body to the other. Actually, this is rather simple when you think of how complicated most students consider blood tracings.

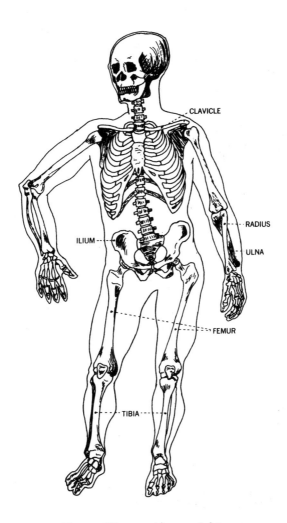

Fig. 5   *Diagram of human skeleton.*

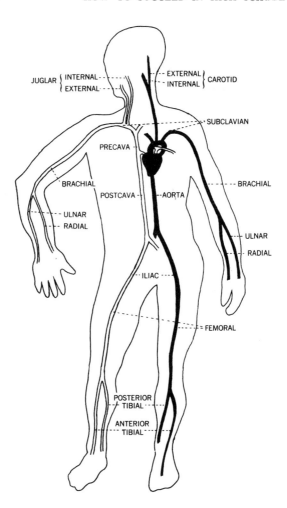

FIG. 6   *Diagrammatic representation of blood system, showing the veins in white* (right side of body) *and arteries in black* (left side of body).

As you continue your study you will learn new organs (of digestion, excretion, reproduction, etc.) All you have to do is learn the name of the blood vessels which supply them and you have another tracing. As was said before, it is easy to learn the fundamentals or rudiments of blood circulation. If you go further into Zoology, as you might if you become a Zoology major, a pre-Medical or pre-Dental student, you will have the basic information on which to build. It can also be pointed out here that other sciences also lend themselves to this same systematic approach. Zoology was used as an illustration only because of its general applicability.

In the process of identifying and learning various structures, bones, organs, etc., you should be making a definite effort to use *Step Three; that is,* you should be trying to *apply* what you know. In the case of the example just given, you should identify the position of each bone, organ, blood vessel *in your own body.* It is difficult to understand *how* a student can learn the bones of the human body and not know where his own *femur* is; but it does happen and with amazing regularity. So, by the time you finish *studying* about the human body you should know something about *your own body.*

There is another reason for identifying the position of various muscles, organs, etc. in and on your own body. Once you know *what* these organs are and their position in your body it is much easier to be able to recall them. It is also easier to identify these same structures in other animals. All you have to do is imagine yourself standing or lying in the same position as the animal in question and you will immediately be able to identify similar structures on that animal. If, for example, you check the very simplified drawing of the skeleton of the Frog (Figure 7) you will immediately see quite a few bones which are similar to the ones listed in the human skeleton.

Students who have had difficulty in learning the circulatory system are quite amazed at how well and how easily they gain mastery of this subject once they use this systematic approach. They do, however, need some assistance in learning how to systematize the learning of future lessons.

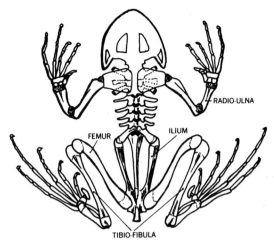

RADIO-ULNA

FEMUR   ILIUM

TIBIO-FIBULA

FIG. 7   *Simplified diagram of skeleton of frog.*

How do you go about systematizing the learning of science courses?

As was stated earlier, *Step one* is to try to get the general idea and the central or main idea of the chapter. To accomplish this you should *read* the chapter without trying to learn or memorize any of the details. In this step you concentrate *only* on getting a general idea of the chapter as well as trying to identify the central idea of the chapter.

Next, *Steps two* and *three* should be applied simultaneously. You should try to use what you have already learned and apply what you are learning to your own body or environment. To help you accomplish your aim of really learning the Biological Sciences, the following steps will be invaluable.

Go over the chapter carefully noting each *italicized* or **BOLD-FACE**-type word. As you look at the word, try to think of any word which will help you to identify or understand what that word means. For example you see the word *iliac* in reference to a vein and to an artery. You already know where the ilium is on the skeleton — so the *iliac* vein should be in the vicinity of the *ilium* — is it? At this point, can you identify where your own *ilium* is? Can you visualize where your own *iliac* vein (artery) runs? Feel your own ilium! Run your finger across your abdomen to trace the path of your own iliac vein (artery). During this process be *sure* you can spell the word. This latter suggestion may seem obvious but in checking Biology examination papers the author has noted *numerous* points lost because of misspelled words.

Now we shall begin to take the chapter apart and put it back together in a way that will force meaningfulness for you. You should note the following things about each *italicized* word.

1] *Definition.*

What does the word mean? Do not memorize the book definition! Put the definition into your own words. If you can explain the definition in your own words you can be reasonably sure you understand the word. Remember, a parrot can memorize a definition but he cannot answer a question about what he has memorized. The importance of getting ideas etc. into your own words has been explained and emphasized elsewhere so we shall not belabor the point.

2] *Function.*

What is the function of this structure (the word you have just learned to define)? In your own words, what does this *thing* do? At this point you have taken a part of the chapter and learned what it is and what it does. Many students take these two steps; but now we are going to put the chapter back together.

3] *Part of.*

What is this organ or structure part of? For example, the *iliac* vein is part of the circulatory system, the blood system and the venous system. What else?

4] *Next to.*

What is the structure next to? Again, the *iliac* vein is next to the *ilium* (general area of the body). It is also next to (connected to) the *inferior vena cava* and next to the *femoral* vein. Notice here that you have a variety of *associations.* You know that the iliac vein is in the vicinity of the ilium. (You will also note that there is an iliac artery) so that, here, the word ilium itself should become meaningful. In addition, you have associations going in two directions, from anterior to posterior and vice versa. If you are tracing a drop of blood *up* one of the limbs you have the association; if the tracing is down you still have the association. This business of associations in two directions is well illustrated by the song *Dry Bones.*

5] *Draw it.*

The last step here is to draw the structure — but draw it correctly. First, you should understand that knowing *how* to draw a structure does *not* involve copying. When you copy you have no way to check yourself to see if you can draw the structure, organ, animal, etc. without the help of the book.

In learning to draw you should train yourself to observe well and see things as they are, quickly and accurately. So, study the structure or picture of it in your book or laboratory manual. Without looking at the structure or picture try to draw it as completely as possible. Now, check your drawing against the original picture or drawing, noting the mistakes and/or omissions you have made. If the drawing you have made is not complete and accurate, *throw it away* and repeat the whole process. Repeat the process until you can reproduce a complete and accurate drawing.

NOTE: This process may at first seem too time-consuming. Experience shows that it is actually the quickest way to learn to make a complete and accurate drawing, and *one which you will be able to retain.*

One other area which should be emphasized in the study of science is the laboratory. Quite often students forget that in the laboratory they are supposed to see and apply what they have learned in the text and/or class. Too often students spend time looking for directions as to what to do – they use the lab manual like a cookbook following one step at a time.

The proper procedure to follow in the laboratory is to *study* the assignment before the class. Study the manual as you study your text book. Now, when you actually go into the lab, spend your time *doing* the work *not* looking up how to do the work.

How can you be expected to spend so much time learning only one subject?

First of all, using this method you will actually spend less time *overall*. It will take you longer to go over your assignment the first time. You will, however, save appreciably in going over and over the same material and in reviews.

Second, the author has been checking this system for years and finds that you should be able to predict about 85% of the questions an instructor will ask on an examination. To be sure, you will not always be able to see the words: Definition, Function, Part of, Next to and Draw it. The question will not be asked in precisely that way but in one way or other this will be the information the instructor wants.

Third and most important! When you learn your science courses in this systematic manner you will *really learn them*. You will have the basic knowledge on which you can build. Continue to work in this fashion and you will get an education with no more effort than it takes the average student to pass a course.

ADDENDUM

As was mentioned previously, the author has been using the system just presented for years. Many students who have used this system with a great deal of success have suggested that, with minor modifications, it has *very* wide applicability. Psychology, Geography, Economics and Sociology are four of the subjects often mentioned which lend themselves to this system of study. Other students have pointed out that they have combined this system with the system for studying Mathematics to study the physical sciences such as Physics and Chemistry. These latter students report that very little modification is needed for those two systems to be extremely helpful in the study of the physical sciences.

These reports are not unusual when one considers the fact that the methods presented are a systematic way of studying. The author suggests that you experiment with applying the method for studying science to the study of physical and social sciences as well as to biological sciences.

CHAPTER **9**

Better English

Just recently one of the author's sons and a group of teen-agers were having a Dixieland Band rehearsal. During a break in the rehearsal the boys were sitting in the living room discussing, among other things, a "creepy" English instructor. It seems that this instructor was attempting to give his students a good background in writing and the students were objecting. Chris Hillyer, one of the boys present, asked the author:

> . . . and why should we have to worry so much about grammatical construction! And, if that's not bad enough this guy has us practicing *similes* and *metaphors* and all that jazz. Nobody cares about that stuff; nobody uses it. Can you show me one place where it does anything for me?

Just a few minutes before the question was asked, Chris had been reading a copy of *Mechanics Illustrated* which he had selected from a stack of the author's automotive magazines. The article he had selected to read was: "Tom McCahill Tests the 1962 Pontiac." Why had he chosen to read McCahill's "test" rather than one of the many other choices available? Let Chris tell his own story —:

> Old Uncle Tom really gives you the scoop on these new cars. He doesn't pull any punches; he says what he means. When you read what he says you get a pretty good idea of the good and bad points of a car. And do you dig those crazy expressions — "like a greased weasle," "like a cannon ball down a chimney," "the XKE is a man's mink coat"! I really get a big charge out of reading his articles.

The author pointed out the fact that Chris had partially answered his own question. In spite of what he had previously said, Chris was impressed by a style of writing and chose to read McCahill's tests rather than others which were available. In fact, the expressions he had singled out as "crazy" and "wild" were examples of what he objected to learning, i.e., *similes* and *metaphors*. Chris was also impressed by the realization that, over the years, all kinds of people from Anthropologists to Zoologists had written to Uncle Tom "an automotive writer," for advice on a variety of subjects. And, these people knew Mr. McCahill *only* through his writing.

It seems unusual that any effort should have to be made to convince students that they should learn and know their own language. But the fact that the college-level, freshman English course is considered by many students as *the* most difficult course shows the need for such emphasis. Students experience a great amount of difficulty with both areas of English: reading and writing. When it is considered that the college-level course assumes twelve years of background in fundamentals, it is easy to see why students have difficulty. The difficulty stems from the fact that students avoid, in fact, object to learning the fundamentals of their own language.

Most students do, however, realize that as educated persons they are expected to be able to express themselves effectively and correctly. Part of the task is overcoming students' aversion to writing and speaking effectively. Some students seem to feel that if they express themselves effectively they are being sissified or affected. Many of these students want to improve their ability to express themselves but just do not know how.

The author's experience has shown that most students want to do better in spite of their objections. During the years of World War II many *hard-boiled* infantrymen came to the author for help in writing letters to former employers and to girl friends they wanted to impress. That persons from "really rough characters" to college students seek help when they want to show themselves off to best advantage should be indication enough that the area of English is important. If not, consider the information which folows.

Mr. Norman Shipley, principal stockholder and managing president of a mineral-pigments company, and a very good friend of the author's, made the following statement in reference to a college industrial engineering program:

> I'm certainly glad to see the English and speech courses in your programs. If it's at all possible I'd like to see even more English and speech. So many of the research chemists and engineers I hire just cannot write a good report. Frequently, I have to go over reports, talk with the researchers and write the report myself; otherwise my board of directors just won't understand why we're asking for money. If I could find a person who understood this work and could write a really good report, he'd be worth a lot of money to me.

In checking with numerous business men, manufacturers, government agencies, etc., this story was repeated over and over. Even so, countless students voice the opinion that English is not very important to them because they are going into some technical area. One of the greatest assets anyone can have is to know how to convey his thoughts or what he knows to others. Mr. Bernard Baruch, one of America's most respected elder statesmen, has said that to be able to express an idea is almost as important as the idea itself.

How can expression of ideas be so important to you now?

As a student you recognize that you must be able to *show* what you have learned in your classes in order to be able to get good grades. In many cases this "showing" will involve writing the answers to examination questions. Later when you apply for college or professional school, or when you apply for a position, in addition to taking entrance and/or placement examinations you may also have to be interviewed. Your ability to express yourself will have a great deal of bearing on whether or not you get into "that school" or get "that job."

You should begin now to do everything in your power to improve your ability to express yourself. Your high school English classes and your classes in public speaking will be of in-estimable value to you — *but*, only if you apply yourself and try to improve.

How can you improve?

The first step in improving is wanting to improve. The second step is realizing that the main purpose in speaking or writing is to get *your* ideas or *your* point of view across to some other person in the clearest and most acceptable form. Regardless of whether you use a humorous, an objective, or a serious way of presenting your ideas, the person with whom you are trying to communicate must understand what you are trying to say.

The next step is for you to recognize that you are a unique individual with unique experiences. Learn to use those experiences and develop a unique way of expressing yourself. You probably have little or no difficulty in talking with and explaining things to your friends. Learn to use that ability.

Just recently, to demonstrate the point that the average student who has difficulty in writing *imagines* much of that difficulty, the author recorded a conversation that was going on among a group of teenagers. Later, he asked each member of the group to write two hundred words on the topic they had been discussing. Each one of these boys objected and said that he could not write a very good "theme" on the topic. The author then played back the tape proving that each one in the group *could* write if he had just listened to what *he himself* had said about the topic.

The following suggestions are the ones the author used in helping many students, including the group just mentioned, to improve their writing ability.

Begin your program for improvement by writing.

It has been the author's experience that most students who experience difficulty in writing do so for three basic reasons: 1] they do not believe that they *can* write, 2] they do not think before they write, and 3] they try to do too many things at one time. It might also be mentioned, at this point, that students also do not capitalize on their basic individual ability to express themselves. But, rather than dwell on the negative side, let us use the very simple plan for improving which has been used so successfully for so many years.

When you are first assigned a topic (or examination question) on which you are to write, — STOP! *Always* look at the topic positively. Ask yourself, what is the best way to approach this topic (or question)? *Never*, for a moment, adopt a negative attitude and suggest to yourself that you cannot write on any topic. The next step is to think of yourself *discussing* the topic with a friend with whom you feel at ease. "Talk" with this friend, explain your ideas to him or her. As you carry on this imaginary conversation, write notes on the points that come to mind. Do not try to be formal, discuss the topic just as naturally as you would discuss it with a friend. Use *your own* expressions and ideas.

After you have finished the discussion, examine your notes. If you have too many ideas to cover in the time or space allotted, cut out the less important topics. If you have too few notes, think of a few more ideas. Now, arrange your notes (ideas) in a logical sequence. Notice that if you follow this system you will almost insure continuity and coherence in your writing. And, these are two of the *big* difficulties students mention: inability to achieve continuity and coherence.

The next step is to think of an opening, something that will "catch" the eye and the "imagination" of the reader. This step should be relatively simple since you *know* what else you are going to write about. By the same token, you should be able to think of an appropriate way to end your little opus.

You should now have an opening, a closing, and a logical *flow* of ideas in between. Check the notes you have made and try to improve on your diction, rhetoric and grammar. The only task left is to write grammatically correct sentences in the same sequence as you have arranged your notes. You will also notice that you have been doing only one thing at a time. You thought of what ideas were to be included, you arranged these ideas in a logical sequence, you chose an appropriate opening and closing, then you were free to concentrate on writing grammatically correct sentences. In other words, you were able to give your full attention to each step and *not* have to try to think of ideas, decide what should come next and how, and write grammatically correct sentences *all at the same time.*

If you are an average student you are probably raising the objection that this procedure takes so long you will have no time to write. This is a common objection. But let us look at how this system works out in actual practice. Students at the university level often find it difficult to write a 250 word in-class theme in a fifty-minute period. The author asks these students: "How long does it take to write 250 words, any 250 words?" The answers vary from fifteen to twenty-five minutes. The student can then see that if he knows *what* words to write he can complete his task in twenty-five to thirty-five minutes. The next step is to have the student follow the "discussion method." The average student checked completes the discussion and rearrangement of notes in ten minutes. And, he is usually quite amazed at how quickly ideas flow when he "turns his head loose" and is not required to write these ideas in *final* form. We find, therefore, in actual practice that the average student (who comes to the author) can write his outline in ten minutes, write his theme in another twenty-five minutes (total thirty-five to forty minutes), and have at least ten minutes to go back, look over, and correct his work.

You may still wish to object. Before you do, try the method. Practice your writing and improve your writing. Unless you learn to express your ideas in a way that others can understand even great ideas may be dormant in your brain and neither you nor others will ever profit from them. Try to get help and suggestions on how to improve from your English instructor. In the meantime, you can also help yourself to improve your *diction, rhetoric* and *grammar* by using the methods suggested in the next sections.

Improve your diction and rhetoric.

Before you attempt any program of improvement it is wise to think about what was said concerning the fact that you are an individual. You have your own unique background, try to *build on* and *improve* your background, do not try to change it or disregard it completely. Next, try to be natural – do not go in for words and expressions which are too unusual or bizarre. But remember, words are your tools and you will have to have a good supply of them to do your job well.

One excellent way of learning new and useful words is to purchase one of the many excellent vocabulary books available at your local book store. You will find the pocket-book THIRTY DAYS TOWARD A MORE POWERFUL VOCABULARY (10) very helpful and convenient. You can carry this little book with you and practice at odd moments during the day and evening. You should, however, also get some real practice on the use, including writing, of these new words. For this purpose, books such as DEVELOPING YOUR VOCABULARY by Paul Witty and Edith Grothberg (25), and CONCERNING WORDS by J. E. Norwood (18), will be extremely useful and helpful. If you are serious about trying to improve, set aside ten or fifteen minutes each day to practice on the work sheets contained in the work books mentioned in this section. Or, if the idea of cards appeals to you, get yourself a box of VIS-ED vocabulary cards and carry a few of them in your pocket. The VIS-ED card idea is a very convenient way to improve your vocabulary.

Another good way of developing your vocabulary is to read. But be selective in your reading. Look around! Choose books by authors who express themselves in the *way you would like to express yourself*. In addition to learning new words you will learn new ways of using expressions. Try *using* the expressions that appeal to you. Select expressions which are as near natural for you as is possible, then use these expressions until they actually become natural for you.

While reading be sure you use your dictionary. You will also find that a copy of ROGET'S THESAURUS (now available in pocket book form) will be very helpful in learning *synonyms* and *antonyms*. It might be wise, at this point, to indicate to you that a good vocabulary will be of *immediate* practical value to you. In addition to helping you to express yourself better, you will find that you will be able to perform better on the vocabulary tests which are an integral part of tests of scholastic aptitude and scholastic achievement. In fact, your ability to perform well on such a test could easily determine your acceptance by the college of your choice.

Learn the rules of grammar and punctuation.

If you want people to understand what you write, you will have to learn to write and punctuate your writing in the generally accepted form. Consider the fact that the two sentences which follow have exactly the same words but different meanings.

> I failed the test; I don't know why I studied for it.
> I failed the test; I don't know why, I studied for it.

One simple comma makes all the difference in meaning. Now, for fun, see if you can punctuate the following group of words so that you understand the meaning:

> time flies you cannot they fly too irregularly

You should be able to see from the very simple illustrations given that the meaning of a group of words can be very drastically changed by correct or incorrect punctuation. You can also see from the next sentences that there might be some doubt about meaning:

I visited my uncle who has two daughters and two hound dogs. They have the ugliest faces I have ever seen.

Since it is impossible to give an English course in a book of this type, suggestions will be made concerning improving your grammar and punctuation. Naturally, the best place to get help is from your high school English teacher. But, if you wish to do the work yourself, here is what is considered by many educators as an excellent way to remedy your difficulty: purchase one of the programmed learning series on English and follow the direction.

There are a great many of these programmed learning texts. Two texts, in particular, have been recommended.

English 2600, Joseph C. Blumenthal (1)
English 3200, Joseph C. Blumenthal (2)

There is one other book (not a programmed text, however) which is an excellent help in vocabulary, rhetoric and grammar, and that is:

A WRITER'S HANDBOOK by D. W. Lee and G. Leggett (13)

Look at the various books suggested and also check your school and local library for additional books. Choose the one *you* feel will be most helpful.

Be observant.

After you have begun your program of improvement BE OB-SERVANT. Be a critic. Learn to catch mistakes made by news-casters and other radio and television personalities. Learn to catch mistakes in books, newspapers, etc. But also, as in your reading, learn to use the new words and modes of expressions that you see and hear.

CHAPTER **10**

Tests and Examinations

How would you rate yourself in the following categories?

1] I get good grades but I would like to be able to get the same grades with less effort and have more time for recreation.

2] I am passing but I would like to get better grades. But, honestly, I just don't have time for additional study. You see I work, etc., etc.

3] I am not really doing well but I know I can't do any better even if I try much harder.

4] Sure I'm just about failing but if I worked hard I'd still get poor grades. I'd rather fail or get "D's" with no work than work hard and get only "C's" and "D's."

Think hard at this point. Maybe no one of the above categories describes you *exactly*. But just about everyone wants to improve, especially if he can do so without too much trouble. In addition, most students would like to be able to take tests without worry and concern and get good grades. How about you?

How do you feel about tests?

Are you one of those students who feels as if he is looking at the business end of a loaded elephant gun each time a teacher announces a test? If so you are not alone. In the book about what college freshmen think (23), examinations were listed as one of the big complaints; in fact, they were referred to as ". . . a terrific strain." Now why should this be? Can *you* give any reasonable answer as to why students should *fear* tests? If you have trouble answering this question, it is because there is no *good* answer. Students who learn how to study and how to take tests soon forget their fears. Some students even look forward to tests and many have learned how to make quizzes, tests and examinations serve several very useful purposes and, in the meantime, get good grades.

If you have been studying well up to this point, it would be sad if you failed to get reasonable grades simply because you were not able to show up to best advantage. The whole secret of how to do your work best (or show up to best advantage) lies in two areas, in your *wanting* to do well and in *knowing how* to do well. Naturally, we cannot make you want to do well; but, if you read and heed the suggestions made in this section, you will improve. How can such results be promised? Simple; studies have been made which show that when a person learns *how to take a test* (nothing else) he will get better grades. It goes without saying that if the same person learns how adequately to prepare for tests he will improve even more.

The author promises you that if you will *learn to apply* what follows in this chapter you will:

1] Forget your test jitters.
2] Get better grades (or get your grades with less effort).
3] Be better able to apply what you are now learning.
4] Learn how to perform better on the various tests and examinations you may be expected to take in or for your vocation.

PREPARING FOR TESTS AND EXAMINATIONS

Do you cram for exams?

In spite of what students learn about how to study and how to distribute their practice (study), there are those individuals who insist on doing a great deal of work (some new and some review) just prior to a test. Have you ever thought of what it would be like to try to cram in a whole week's practice for Saturday's game on Friday afternoon and evening? Or of what it would be like to do *all* of your practice on a musical instrument the day before your recital? The chances are that by the time you began your third or fourth hour of practice you would be tired of and disgusted from practicing. But in either case you would be either so tired or so stale you would not perform very well. Knowing these facts, are you still one of those students who ignores what he knows and still crams for tests?

You already know something about reviewing but let us look at suggestions already made in a different light. Let us look at studying in the same way we would look at practicing for the big game or for that recital. First, try to practice (study) each day; review what you have learned each week (each two weeks, each month, etc.); relax the night before the game (test); warm up before the test; then go over the rules of how you are to take your examination (these rules will be discussed later in this chapter) so that you can start your test *the minute the test is placed on your desk.*

How would you review specifically for a test?

Since you have been using the SARTOR method in your studying, you will need only a few short, periodic reviews of what you have already overlearned to be ready for your next test. In fact, it has been stated over and over, even at the graduate level in universities, that a student who studies efficiently should not have to spend more than one hour reviewing for any test or examination. Once material has been overlearned, a brief review is all that is necessary to keep the material on the "tip of your tongue."

First, go back over the schedule you made (Schedule Sheet) and set aside some review time for each subject each week. How much time? Well, the amount will depend on you, the subject, how well you have learned and overlearned, and on how much you will have to relearn. Try reviewing each of your subjects at the end of a week to figure out for yourself just how much time will be needed. This process will necessitate periodic changes in your schedule so that you can keep up with your daily work *and* your reviews. When you follow this procedure you will be prepared for every class recitation, for every "pop test," and *you will have little or no reviewing to do the night before any announced test.* Many college students in the author's effective-study course mention this suggestion as *the most valuable of all suggestions.*

Please understand, however, that no one can show you precisely how to set up the schedule which will be best for you. *You* must work on your own schedule keeping in mind *your* needs and how much time *you* will have available and when it is available. In all reviews, focus attention on practicing what you expect to do later and *apply* what you have learned. If you have to recite before a group, practice *reciting*; if you have to answer questions, practicing *answering*; if you have a performance class (such as shop, serving, art, etc.) practice *performing* — practice *doing* what you will be asked to do. But above all, prepare *well* and completely. Do not try to second-guess the teacher on *precisely what kinds of questions* you will be given; prepare for *all kinds of questions.*

What about confidence in taking tests?

If you prepare as has been suggested you can go into any test as confident as if you were allowed to take all your books with you. In fact, you can be *more* confident. Sound peculiar? Not at all. Actually, when you go into a test *well-prepared* you have all the information and facts in your head where they are readily available. With a book or list of questions and answers (crib) you would be constantly looking back and forth, turning pages, etc., etc. When the questions and answers are in your head, you have an *immediate* reference — no waste of time (high school students often mention that *this* suggestion is *the most valuable one*). And nothing will give you more confidence in your preparation than picking up a test and seeing a list of questions you have answered several times.

Now, when you learn how to use what you know, *how to take a test*, there will be *nothing* to keep you from getting good grades — *easily*.

One word of caution relative to your questions should be mentioned at this point. Several students who have tried this system have reported that they ran into difficulty. But their difficulty can be summarized very simply. These students looked for *exactly* the same questions they had in their notebooks; in fact, some of these students expected the *same words* and same *phraseology*! Do not fall into that *trap*! Naturally, the teacher will word and phrase questions differently from the way you do. When you see or hear the teacher's question, ask yourself what information he wants — do not worry about the form of the question or the words he uses. Take the following three questions, all of which ask for the same fact, as examples of what is meant:

————————————, a famous figure of Colonial times, is reported to have thrown a ————————— across the ————————— River.

George Washington is reported to have performed a feat which would cause any big-league center fielder to marvel. Describe that feat.

It is said that in Colonial times a "dollar went much farther than it does today." Describe an incident in the life of George Washington which might humorously illustrate that saying.

These three differently-phrased questions asked for the same facts. Any student reading this section can probably think of many additional questions which would also ask for these same facts. If you will use this ability when you review, it will be difficult for any teacher to make up questions you have not already seen and answered.

TAKING TESTS AND EXAMINATIONS

How do you take a test?

If you want a good picture of yourself taking a test, observe a group of your friends when they are given a test. You will see confusion, suppressed panic, fear, and possibly some cool, calculated work. Te⁻ to fifteen minutes or possibly a half hour after the test has been distributed, most of the students are fairly well calmed down and working reasonably well. If, however, you watch a group of students who have been taught how to take a test, you will see an entirely different picture. When the tests are distributed the students immediately begin to work — no fuss, no confusion and no ten-to-fifteen minute warm-up period. Students who have learned how to take tests begin immediately because they know what they are going to do and how to do it. They have a plan for taking tests and they waste no effort.

Do you know how to take a test?

Literally thousands of students who have prepared for their tests fail to show up to best advantage simply because they do not know *how* to use what they have learned. In addition, they do not know how to make the *best* use of their time.

If, at this point, you were asked how to take an essay or objective test, could you outline a plan which would make the best use of what you know in the shortest time possible? Unless you have been taught how to take tests, the answer is probably, no! Of course, you know how to take a test, but do you know the *best way?*

In order for you to do well on any test, you must be prepared. And, there is only one kind of preparation, thorough preparation. But being well-prepared means more than studying before a test. You must, in addition, be psychologically prepared for that test. You must know that when you walk into your test you will be like a track star getting on his mark, set to start a race. There will be a certain amount of *nervous anticipation,* but do not mistake this reaction for fear or jitters. The feeling of anticipation will mean that you are ready and waiting to go. Now, when the test is placed on your desk you should know exactly how to begin. You should have a system for each different kind of test.

How should you take a test?

1] *Arrive* at the designated place at least ten minutes before the test is scheduled to begin. Be sure you have allowed yourself time to take care of *all* last minute details. There should be no "rushing around" — rushing usually excites one and an excited person is not in any condition to do his best work. At this point, there is no need to discuss the test with your fellow students. If you do talk with your friends, discuss something that is far removed from school and studies. You have prepared well; there is no need for last minute discussions. If you are allowed, sit near the front of the room so you will get your paper first; this procedure will ordinarily give you a few extra minutes for additional work. Now, check around to find if there have been any last-minute changes. Listen *carefully* to the directions the teacher gives before she passes out the test.

Now you have the test.

2] *Scan* the whole test. How many questions, sections, sheets are there? Read the directions for the whole test and for each section of the test — *Read the directions carefully, very* carefully. This procedure will give you a rough idea of the length and difficulty of the test. Do not allow yourself to pay attention to any one question. Just find out how much there is to do. Be sure of this last step. Students *often* accidentally skip questions and even whole pages or sections, and often fail to make time for questions which count for many points.

3] *Plan* your time according to the number of questions or sections *and the point value of each question or section.* For example — Suppose you have five essay questions (*each worth twenty points*) to complete in fifty minutes. You allow yourself ten minutes for each question. Suppose, on the other hand, you have a recognition type test with fifty true-false questions (worth twenty-five points), and twenty-five single-choice questions (worth seventy-five points). You allow about *twelve minutes* for the whole T-F section and about thirty-five minutes for the single-choice section.

4] *Start* your test —

Have you read the directions carefully? Do you know how the T-F items should be marked? In the *choice* items, are you to choose the *best* answer, the *correct* answer(s), the *incorrect* answer(s)? Do you know that some teachers will count a whole section as *wrong* if directions are not followed *exactly?* Be sure that you have read the directions *carefully* — and that now you *follow the directions exactly!*

Each type of test requires a different technique if you are going to get the best score with what you know. Let us begin by looking at what are called *Recognition* tests. Your teacher may refer to them as *Objective Tests.* In these tests you are not asked to *recall* answers. You are, however, asked to *recognize* correct and incorrect answers. Let us look at the various types of recognition tests and the procedures for taking each type.

RECOGNITION TESTS

True-false tests.

EXAMPLE: T-F. Billy the Kid is the well-known mascot of the U.S.N.A.

In a true-false test, reading and following the directions can make a great difference in your score. Ordinarily, these tests are graded or scored by subtracting the number of wrong answers from the number of correct answers (Score = Rights — Wrongs). If your teacher uses this system let us see what happens on a one hundred-point test. Suppose you *know* seventy-five of the items and get them correct. Suppose also you guess at the remaining twenty-five and guess wrong. Your score would be S = 75 − 25 or 50. Suppose, however, you did not guess and left the remaining 25 blank. Your score would be 75 − 0 or 75. Quite a difference! On the other hand, if your teacher does not subtract the wrong answers, your score in the example given above would still be 75. A good general rule to follow is: if there is no penalty for wrong answers, guess at the answers you do not know.

Now in taking your T-F test, plan to follow this procedure —

1) Read the first statement quickly but carefully and decide immediately whether it is *true or false*. Record your answer and *do not change it*. Research shows that for each question you change from incorrect to correct, you will change approximately three from correct to incorrect. In other words, the odds are three to one *against* you if you change an answer.

2) Suppose, however, that after reading the statement you are not *sure* the statement is true or false; but you *think* you know — you have a *hunch*. Play that hunch, record the answer and, again, do not change it. Playing a hunch is not the same as guessing. Often, because you have read the text and have listened in class, you will feel or think a statement is true or false without knowing *why*. Play your hunch because the odds are in your favor that you will answer correctly.

   One simple rule will help you in deciding whether a statement is true or false: T-F items which contain modifiers such as always or never are *usually* false. It is very difficult to write a statement for a test which is *always* true or *never* false. Try this statement for fun.

   T-F.   Items which contain modifiers such as always or never are always false.

3) If you do not know whether the statement is true or false, have no idea or hunch, leave the statement blank, skip it. Do not spend time working on or thinking about such items, go immediately to the next statement. True-false tests are usually set up in such a way that if you spend too much time on any one statement, you will not have time to finish the test. Notice that when you follow this procedure you are spending your time on what you *do* know and not wasting your time on items which you are very dubious about or know nothing about.

4) If, after you have finished the remainder of the test

(not just the T-F section) you still have a few minutes to work, you may want to go back over the T-F section. If there is no penalty for wrong answers — guess — do not leave any blanks. If there is a penalty for incorrect answers, again follow the same procedures listed above under 1, 2, 3, and 4. Later, when you read the section on how to take Essay tests you will see why this suggestion is made and how it works.

Single-choice tests.

EXAMPLE: *Pizzicato* refers to:

    (*a*)   a small Italian tomato pie
    (*b*)   a famous leaning tower
    (*c*)   plucked strings
    (*d*)   a small gnome-like figure

In this type of test you are asked to make a *single* choice. You may be asked for the *correct* answer, the *best* answer or the *incorrect* answer. In any event you have a single choice, and you should handle the items in the manner described below.

A] Read the statement and try to recall the correct answer, see if the answer you recalled is listed among the choices and mark it immediately. If you were not able to recall the correct answer, but on the *first* reading of the choices you *recognize* the correct answer, mark it *immediately*. If you cannot answer the question *on the first reading*, immediately go on to the next question. Again you will be spending your time on what you do know.

    If you are to choose the best answer or incorrect answer follow the same procedure. Where you are to choose the *best* answer, compare the answer you have recalled with the choices given. If you are to chose the incorrect answer, compare the answer(s) you recalled with the choices given in order to help you to decide on which is the incorrect answer.

The secret, however, of taking this type of test is to decide immediately whether or not you know the answer. If you cannot decide *right now*, go on to the next item so that you do not waste time. In addition, when you read the section on Essay tests, you will learn how this procedure will put your memory to work for you.

B]   If you have followed the suggestions given in section "A." above, you should have time to go back and check some of the statements you failed to complete on the first round. (Should you not have time for a second round, you can at least be sure that you spent your time to best advantage. That is you spent your time on what you knew, not wasting time guessing.)

On the second round you will immediately *recognize* the answers to some of the questions you skipped. In that case follow the directions given under "A." above. For the items you still do not recognize, follow one or both of the procedures listed below to help you to recognize the correct answer.

1) Eliminate the obviously incorrect answers to help to reduce the odds against you, e.g.

The father of psychoanalysis was:

  (*a*)   William James
  (*b*)   George Washington
  (*c*)   Sigmund Freud
  (*d*)   Henry Clay

You may not know a thing about psychoanalysis but certainly you can eliminate the names of George Washington and Henry Clay. You have bettered your odds. Your chances are now one-in-two instead of one-in-four.

2) If, after you have tried the suggestions listed above, and you still have time, you may find it helpful to treat the single-choice items as true-false items.

e.g., The father of psychoanalysis was William James. (T-F).

The father of psychoanalysis was Sigmund Freud.
(T-F).
Often just combining the statement with the choice
will ring a bell for you and you will recognize the correct answer.

Multiple-choice tests.

EXAMPLE:
Examinations are usually designed to accomplish the following purposes:

(*a*) To motivate study
(*b*) To instill fear in students
(*c*) To help students to learn how to apply what they
have learned.
(*d*) To help teachers to vent their aggression.

Although multiple-choice items are usually considerably
more difficult than single-choice items, the system for taking
such tests is quite simple. In taking such a test you must remember that each item of four choices actually constitutes
four true-false items. Consequently, a test with 100 mulitple
choice items actually contains *400 true-false* items. And, like
a true-false test, you are usually penalized for errors. Therefore,
the easiest, quickest and most efficient way to take a multiple-
choice test is to treat it like a T-F test. Read the statement
with the first choice and decide immediately whether it is
true or false. Now, it is all according to the directions how
you proceed from this point. If you are supposed to indicate
correct answers, you check those which are true. You follow
these same directions for each successive choice being sure you
read the whole statement with each choice. This procedure
makes it easier to make the correct association. Do not rely on
what you *think* the statement was, *read* it with each choice.

Since, in multiple-choice tests, you are usually penalized for
incorrect answers, it usually helps a student to know what happens when he leaves a blank. A blank can be correct or incorrect according to the directions. To clarify this statement, let

us refer to the example given at the beginning of the *Multiple-choice* section. Suppose you honestly do not know whether choice (*b*) is a correct or incorrect choice — you cannot even guess, so you do not check an answer. If the directions called for you to check *correct* answers, you would have received credit. On the other hand, if you had been asked to check *incorrect* answers, you would have been wrong (since (*b*) is an incorrect answer). So, without going into further instructions, your best bet is to treat multiple choice tests exactly the way you treat T-F items.

Matching tests.

Matching Tests usually consist of two lists, one of facts, events or persons, and the other of descriptions, explanations or dates. The students' task is to match an item from the first list with the appropriate item from the second list. While most high school students are familiar with these tests, they take them in such a way that the *Matching Test* is a notorious time-consumer. If you will follow the one simple direction given below you will find that your task will be greatly simplified.

In your next *Matching Test*, read *both* lists carefully and completely before you check *any* answers. This procedure will help you to find the most obvious matches immediately and eliminate the necessity for changing answers when you find a *better* match later. You will also find that this procedure will make use of the memory factor which has been mentioned so often and which will be discussed in the section on essay tests which follows immediately.

RECALL TESTS

Essay tests.

EXAMPLE: Discuss completely the following statement: Since young men eighteen years of age are expected to serve in the Armed Forces in times of national emergency, they should be given the right to vote.

As you can well imagine, only a few questions such as th

one given in the example above could be covered in the usual test period. Therefore, we shall consider essay tests as those which contain relatively few questions and require relatively long answers written in your own words.

Before we begin the discussion on how to take essay tests, ask yourself two questions. How many times have you walked out of a test room and found that ten or twenty minutes later you recalled the answer to one of the questions you could not get on the test? Or, how many times have you written at the end of your test: "no time to finish"? If you plead guilty to either of these faults, you are using improper methods of taking tests. Let us see how you should procede so that you will eliminate these faults.

1) Read and follow the general directions. If the teacher asks you to answer 4 out of 5 questions, make up your mind to answer *4 questions. Follow the directions.*

2) Read *all* of the questions before answering any one question. Decide how much time each answer should get. If, for example, you have five twenty-point questions to answer in fifty minutes, you should allot ten minutes to each answer. Now, which question will be the *easiest* for you to answer? Suppose, after reading all five questions you decide three will be easy to answer, one you know but cannot recall, and you know *nothing at all* about the last one, or at least you cannot recall the answer for it.

You should now be ready to begin with the *easiest* question, remembering that you are going to stick to your time schedule. Remember, if you adhere to your time schedule you will have time to write *something* about each question and will not have to write those sad words, *no time to finish.* In addition, students usually get the greater number of points in the early stages of the answer to any essay question regardless of how much they know about the particular topic. Therefore, writing and writing to wring out every last point usually results in wasted time.

3) Begin with the *easiest.* But, before you start to write, take a minute or so to *plan* your answer – outline it if pos-

sible, as suggested in Chapter 8. Most students object to this suggestion saying they do not have time to plan and outline. Actually, this suggestion will help to *save* time and to write a better answer. In most essay tests you are graded on *how well you present facts.* When a student begins to write *without* thinking, he usually finds that he does not have his facts in a logical sequence, nor can he think of suitable ways of connecting facts in a readable way. Stopping, correcting and rearranging take more time than planning. Also, there is the fact that a patched-up answer is never as good as a well-planned one.

Stop when you have given this answer its allotted time!

4) Now begin your second-best answer. Begin each answer on a fresh sheet of paper so that if you have time and wish to add to the previous answer, you will have space to do so.

Since you read *all* of the questions before you began to write, you will ordinarily have an unusual experience some ten to fifteen minutes after the test begins. Essay questions are usually related to each other in a variety of ways and you will find that while writing one answer additional thoughts will occur to you. The answers or facts you knew but could not recall will occur to you while you are writing in the same way the same answers or facts occur to you ten or twenty minutes *after* you have finished the test. In this case, however, you recalled the answer while there is still time to use it. *Stop!* Write a brief outline of the answer you just recalled or jot down the facts, then go back to finish the answer on which you had been working. But please remember to write what you just recalled because otherwise, under the pressure of the test you *might forget* the answer just when you *need* it. But then it is always a good idea to jot down ideas as they occur to you and *not* trust your memory.

(You will find that this suggestion given above will help explain why it was suggested that you go through objective examinations as quickly as possible. Many times after you have read a question or item the answer will occur to you *after* you have stopped thinking about it. The object is to read as many of those questions as quickly as possible so that your head can go to work for you and recall the answers while you are still taking the test.)

5) Now, let us suppose you have finished every question you knew and have recalled, but there is still one question about which you know nothing. What do you do? Simple — you just begin to write — write anything that comes into your head, and try to write for the ten minutes you have allotted to that answer. This suggestion is often looked upon with some suspicion by students and teachers alike but only because they do not understand the reasoning behind it. First, seldom, *if ever,* can a teacher ask a question about which you know absolutely nothing — that is, if you have been to class and have done your assignments — and especially if you have followed the study hints given in this book. Second, the author has found that very often students only *think* they do not know the answer or they say they do not (did not) know *enough* to write a satisfactory answer. These same students almost invariably report that they pick up enough extra points when following this suggestion to make the time well-spent. Remember, if you leave an essay question blank, you get a zero. If you write a *completely wrong* answer, the lowest grade you can get is a zero, so there is no penalty for a wrong answer. When there is no penalty for wrong answers (and you do not know the answer), always try.

6) If you have completed your test and have a few minutes remaining, read over your answers and try to *improve* them.

Short-answer tests.

EXAMPLE:

1] Name five military men prominent in the American Revolution.
2] Describe in one sentence how a student should overlearn a poem.

Often a teacher will give a test consisting of thirty or forty questions allowing you only one to three minutes to complete each answer. In this type of test you will not have time to read all questions before you begin to write. You, therefore, follow a procedure similar to the one suggested for taking single-choice tests.

A] Read the question and write the answer as quickly as possible.

B] If you cannot answer the question *immediately*, skip it and go to the next question.

c] Go through the entire test answering those questions you know as quickly yet as carefully as possible. Remember, each question is worth only so many points and consequently worth only so many minutes. Skip all questions you do not know, are uncertain about, and those where you will have to stop and think for a few moments.

D] Now go back and work over the questions you have skipped using the same procedure used in A, B, and c. You will find that you have recalled the answers to quite a few of the questions you did not know — will be much more certain about some of the questions where you had doubt — and will be able to write the answers (quickly) to some questions on which you previously would have had to give considerable thought.

Mathematics test.

A Mathematics test should be handled just like an essay-type test or short-answer type test according to the one it resembles. If, for example, your Mathematics test consists of three, four, or five problems such as the demonstration problem used in the Mathematics section of this text, you use exactly the same procedure suggested for essay-type examinations. In using this procedure, however, several additional suggestions are necessary. First, if you find that after beginning a problem you become "stuck," go to the next problem. Do not spend *too much time* on one step of the problem. Then come back to this same problem a few minutes later, after you have completed the others you *can do quickly*. Second, it is necessary for you to know how your instructor grades. For example: does your instructor give part credit for setting up the problem? — part credit for all work done? — and part credit for the *correct* answer? Or, are you graded entirely on the answer? Naturally, you will have to plan your work according to how the instructor grades. Third, if you find a problem about which you know absolutely nothing, cannot even start it, then you must skip this problem. It would be difficult to do as was suggested in essay-type tests: just write. Instead it is suggested that you use the time you would have spent on this problem in *checking* (*proving*) the answers and work you have already completed.

When, on the other hand, your teacher may give thirty or forty problems.

EXAMPLE:

A) Multiply $\dfrac{8}{x^2 - 5} \cdot \dfrac{3x + 4}{22} =$

B) Solve for x $\dfrac{4x + 3}{7} - \dfrac{x + 7}{3} = 5$

c) Simplify $\sqrt{63}$

With this type of test you simply follow the directions given for a short-answer type test.

What can I do to help me to perform better on tests?

1) Outline the procedure you are going to use for each kind of test:

A]	True-false test	E]	Matching test
B]	Single-choice test	F]	Short-answer test
c]	Multiple-choice test	G]	Mathematics test
D]	Essay test		

2) Make sure that when you are asked a question you know what the teacher wants. To help you do this look up the

definitions of the following words which are often used on tests and often misunderstood or misinterpreted:

A] list	G] explain
B] compare	H] enumerate
C] contrast	I] (and any additional words you
D] describe	have found on other tests you
E] evaluate	have taken.)
F] criticize	

3) Ask your teacher approximately how many tests he will give and when they will be given. Revise your time schedule so that you will have ample review time for all tests.

In addition you could:

4) Revise your notebook to provide a review section to consist of *all* the questions you can get on each section of each subject you have studied — provide space for the answers to these questions.

5) Plan to revise and correct *all* returned tests.

AND

6) Consult with your teacher to discover where you made your mistakes and how you can correct them.

BIBLIOGRAPHY

1. Bleifeld, M., *How to Prepare for College Board Achievement Tests — Biology*, Barron's Educational Series, (Woodbury, N. Y., 1973).
2. Blumenthal, J. C., *English 2600*, Rev. ed., Harcourt, Brace, and World, Inc., (New York, 1962).
3. Blumenthal, J. C., *English 3200*, Harcourt, Brace, and World, Inc., (New York, 1962).
4. Brownstein, S., *Barron's Mathematics Workbook for College Entrance Examinations*, Barron's Educational Series, (Woodbury, N. Y., 1971).
5. Brownstein, S., *College Bound*, 4th Rev. ed., Barron's Educational Series, (Woodbury, N. Y., 1971).
6. Brownstein, S. and M. Weiner, *Barron's How to Prepare for College Entrance Examinations*, 4th Rev. ed., Barron's Educational Series, (Woodbury, N. Y., 1972).
7. Cabat, L. and J. D. Godin, *How to Prepare for College Board Achievement Tests — French*, Barron's Educational Series, (Woodbury, N. Y., 1971).
8. Cabat, L. and J. D. Godin, *How to Prepare for College Board Achievement Tests — Spanish*, Barron's Educational Series, (Woodbury, N. Y., 1971).
9. Crowder, N. A. and G. Martin, *Adventures in Algebra*, Tutor text, Doubleday and Company, Inc., (Garden City, L. I., 1960).
10. Funk, W. and N. Lewis, *Thirty Days Toward a More Powerful Vocabulary*, Funk and Wagnalls, (New York, 1942). Also available in pocketbook.
11. Gerwig, A., *How to Prepare for College Board Achievement Tests — Latin*, Barron's Educational Series, (Woodbury, N. Y., 1965).
12. Gewirtz, H., *How to Prepare for College Board Achievement Tests — Physics*, Barron's Educational Series, (Woodbury, N. Y., 1963).

13. Lee, D. W. and G. Leggett, *A Writer's Handbook*, Prentice-Hall, Inc., (New York, N. Y., 1954).

14. Midgley, D. A., *How to Prepare for College Board Achievement Tests — Social Studies*, Barron's Educational Series, (Woodbury, N. Y., 1974).

15. Murphy, D. P., *Temac, First Year Algebra*, Encyclopedia Britannica Films, Inc., (1960).

16. Newmark, N. and P. Scherer, *How to Prepare for College Board Achievement Tests — German*, Barron's Educational Series, (Woodbury, N. Y., 1973).

17. Newsom, C. V. and H. Eves, *An Introduction to College Mathematics*, Prentice-Hall, Inc., (New York, N. Y., 1954).

18. Norwood, J. E., *Concerning Words*, Prentice-Hall, Inc., (New York, N. Y., 1950).

19. Polya, G., *How To Solve It*, Princeton University Press, (Princeton, N. J., 1945). Also available in pocketbook form, Doubleday and Company, Inc., (Garden City, N. Y.).

20. Robinson, F. P., *Effective Study*, Harper and Brothers (New York, 1941).

21. Shostak, J., *How to Prepare for College Board Achievement Tests — English*, Barron's Educational Series, (Woodbury, N. Y., 1969).

22. Mascetta, Joseph A., *How to Prepare for College Board Achievement Tests—Chemistry*, Barron's Educational Series, (Woodbury, N. Y., 1969).

23. Townsend, Agatha, *College Freshmen Speak Out*, Harper and Brothers (New York, 1956).

24. Weigand, G. and W. S. Blake, *College Orientation*, Prentice-Hall, Inc., (Englewood Cliffs, N. J., 1955).

25. Witty, P. and E. Grothberg, *Developing Your Vocabulary*, Science Research Associates, Inc., (Chicago, Ill., 1960).

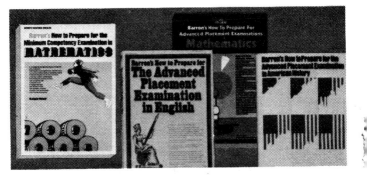

How to Prepare for the Minimum Competency Examination: Mathematics

Angelo Wieland   256 pp., $7.95

A thorough and authoritative volume with complete coverage of all the math syllabus topics, summaries of key concepts, a generous amount of worked-out examples and exercises, and 3 model exams (a diagnostic test and two practice tests) with answers.

How to Prepare for the Regents Competency Test in Reading

Fredericks and Lipner
340 pp. $6.95

Provides thorough instruction in reading the various types of passages found on the exam, with numerous explained examples. The book opens with a full-length diagnostic test and concludes with 2 complete model exams; answers are explained. Hundreds of practice exercises.

How to Prepare for the Regents Competency Test in Writing

Leon Gersten   340 pp., $6.95

Dozens of examples clearly illustrate good and bad writing techniques. Includes special instruction in the most effective method of organizing ideas for writing, plus a diagnostic test and two full-length practice tests.

How to Prepare for the Advanced Placement Examinations in English

Nadel and Sherrer   320 pp. $6.95

Preparation for the Advanced Placement Examinations in English literature including 3 sample tests simulating the style and emphasis of the actual exam. Covers essay and multiple-choice type questions.

How to Prepare for the Advanced Placement Examinations in Mathematics

Shirley O. Hockett   480 pp. $9.95

Comprehensive review and self-testing guide for the first year of calculus. Covers syllabi for Calculus AB and Calculus BC exams. Includes four practice tests with answers.

How to Prepare for the Advanced Placement Examinations in American History

William O. Kellogg   320 pp.. $6.95

Complete course guide for advanced placement and academic enrichment classes. Contains 8 review units with essay and multiple-choice questions; work in essay preparation, vocabulary-building, current affairs, anthologies of key documents and readings; and a model Advanced Placement examination simulating the actual AP test.

BARRON'S TEST PREP BOOKS.

BARRON'S MINIMUM COMPETENCY and ADVANCED PLACEMENT BOOKS

How to Prepare for the Minimum Competency Examination in Mathematics $7.95

How to Prepare for the Regents Competency Examination in Reading $6.95

How to Prepare for the Regents Competency Examination in Writing $6.95

How to Prepare for the Advanced Placement Examination: American History $6.95/Biology $6.95/English $6.95/Mathematics $9.95

SAT (Scholastic Aptitude Test)

How to Prepare for the College Entrance Examinations (SAT) $7.95

Basic Tips on the SAT $3.50

Math Workbook for SAT $6.95   Verbal Workbook $5.95

601 Words You Need to Know for the SAT, PSAT, GRE, State Regents, and other Standardized Tests $5.50

CBAT (College Board Achievement Test)

American History/Social Studies $7.95/Biology $7.95/Chemistry $7.95/English $6.95/European History and World Cultures $7.95/French $7.95/German $5.95/Latin $5.95/Math Level I $7.95/Math Level II $7.95/Physics $6.95/Spanish $8.95

ACT (American College Testing Program)

How to Prepare for the American College Testing Program (ACT) $7.95

Basic Tips on the ACT $3.50

PSAT/NMSQT (Preliminary Scholastic Aptitude Test/National Merit Scholarship Qualifying Test)

How to Prepare for the PSAT/NMSQT $6.95

Basic Tips on the PSAT/NMSQT $3.50

Books may be purchased at your local bookstore, or by mail directly from Barron's. Enclose check or money order for total amount plus sales tax where applicable and 15% for postage and handling (mininum charge $1.50). All books are paperback editions.